How to Make
Virtual Engagement Easy

This book is based on 100+ videos. Below are just a few of the thousands of comments left by leaders and educators on the content you are about to read.

Vicki   2 days ago

I have been a communication trainer for 34 years. I've worked mostly solo for 33 of them. That has offered me a lot of freedom, but not much opportunity for collaborative thinking. Your tools and videos have been a boon for me. They are excellent: immediately actionable, entertaining, useful and fun. They have helped me add new thinking and energy into my training. Thank you for your excellence and generosity.

      REPLY

Robinson   3 weeks ago

Love these videos, Chad! I've been doing a lot of remote workshops/meetings and I love coming to your channel to get tips, techniques and just learn! Keep it going.

         REPLY

Steve 5 hours ago

Of all of the (instructional) videos I have ever seen on YouTube ... about online meetings, this video has been a combination of the most helpful, the most engaging, and the most fun to watch. Great job!

    REPLY

Corrine 1 day ago

After raving about your videos last week to colleagues, I'm sharing with them as well. Thank you for the inspiration you and your company have provided for me during this pandemic. I'm enjoying the book and sad that it's quickly coming to a close for me. I use the *We! Connect Cards* all the time and would love to see the new deck that your team has been working on. Thank you!

    REPLY

Carla 4 days ago

We and Me has planted a seed in me to get rid of disconnected "icebreakers" and embrace connection before content!

    REPLY

Lorie 2 weeks ago

We and Me always provides me with thoughts to ponder, strategies I can use, and most of all inspires me to keep on striving to be the best teacher I can be. Thank you!

   REPLY

 Lisa 1 month ago

One thing I learned from Chad and Will about how to make virtual connection better: the value in helping participants connect to the purpose of why they're there. And I love the aspiration to make online work *better than* being in person!

   REPLY

 Jeff 2 hours ago

Chad, your videos are a wonderful infusion of inspiration and ideas for creating engaging virtual interactions. Thanks so much for sharing them with us! I've been doing this work for a long time and continue to pull nuggets of value from each video I watch.

   REPLY

HOW TO MAKE
VIRTUAL
ENGAGEMENT
EASY

A Practical Guide for Remote
Leaders and Educators

CHAD LiTTLEFiELD
WiLL WiSE

Edited by Michael Schroeder
Cover and layout design by Victoria Dickson

Packaged by We and Me, Inc.
Pittsburgh, PA

Printed in the United States of America
ISBN: 978-0-9964239-5-3
Library of Congress Control Number: 2021921118
North Charleston, SC

As James Joyce once said,

"Mistakes are the portals of discovery."

Without my fumbles and failures,
I would never have stumbled upon the many
best practices and lessons I share in this book.

—Chad Littlefield

Read me first!

Table of Contents

You'll notice this table of contents is a whole heap longer and more detailed than other books. This is to give you a quick, scannable reference guide to the strategies, tips and activities that are most relevant for you.

In fact, we'd encourage you to follow your curiosity and read the book out of order. Each chapter is written to stand completely on its own.

5 ESSENTIAL INGREDIENTS FOR ENGAGEMENT

VIRTUAL ACTIVITIES

ONLINE LEARNING

Who is this book for?

After years of working with some of the smartest leaders and the most creative educators on the planet, we became obsessed with creating tools and resources to help make their jobs easier while increasing their impact. This book is for all those leaders and educators who know that part of changing their world involves investing in themselves and their own learning.

If you want to increase connection and engagement among your staff and students, this is your resource.

Through our work with some of the top universities and organizations, we've noticed that the concepts and strategies in this book really benefit professional facilitators, corporate trainers, educators and coaches. Anybody who has been "voluntold" to lead a meeting or kick off a retreat with an icebreaker will also soak this book up like a sponge.

While we chose to focus on virtual and remote connection and engagement here, so many of the concepts apply beautifully to in-person collaboration as well. What you'll learn will help you work smarter remotely and allow you to have a much greater impact with your teams, classes and audiences.

Foreword

As a higher education professional working in the midst of a global pandemic, I found Chad's depth of knowledge about virtual engagement to be invaluable and reassuring. His steadfast commitment to engagement was evident even in his voicemail. *"Hey there, you've reached Chad. Leave your contact information along with one interesting thing about you that I don't already know. Make it a great day!"*

At the start of 2020, if you'd told me that new student orientation at North Dakota State University would need to fully transition to an online format in less than six weeks, I would've said that wasn't possible. However, as so many of our lived experiences during the pandemic have demonstrated, we can do a lot when there is no alternative.

This quick transition forced us to ask the question, "What is the most important thing for incoming students to gain from their orientation experience?" Time and again the answer was that we needed an opportunity to develop connection. It quickly became clear that we couldn't accomplish this with a traditional online presentation or meeting. As a department, we determined that collaborating with someone who had expertise in promoting virtual connection would be essential as we shifted to an online orientation.

Chad's vision and deep knowledge in this area were critical, as he helped us develop a comprehensive programmatic plan for virtually engaging students. During a staff meeting, our administrative assistant shared that her daughters had attended their virtual new student orientation, and had been nervous about it beforehand. She beamed with pride when she said that they loved their orientation, and had both left with contact information for potential new friends. It was empowering to hear that although our delivery method had changed, our outcomes could remain the same as long as we had effective virtual engagement strategies.

I am confident that as you read through this book, you'll be able to envision how you, too, can implement virtual engagement strategies to achieve your learning and organizational outcomes. College students are some of the toughest critics of virtual engagement because they understand the virtual world so well.

The student staff I work with have put their stamp of approval on Chad's practical methods for making virtual engagement easy. Prior to the start of summer orientation, our student staff had the opportunity to present their online workshop to faculty and staff across campus. Attendees shared that after seeing the presentation, they planned to utilize these same virtual connection activities with their professional staff.

"Chad helps you remember to make connections rather than just diving into content," an intern in our office shared. "And that makes all the difference."

As you explore all the practical insights this book has to offer, my hope is that you'll feel empowered to engage your own creativity to effectively navigate virtual meeting spaces. We all have the opportunity each day to be a connector and engage others we work with virtually or face-to-face.

This book is a tool to help you do just that. I look forward to the day when I can meet Chad in person to get a signed copy of his work.

Yes, you read that right. I have never connected with Chad outside the virtual world. My experience is a serendipitous testament to the value of "connection before content." Make it a great day and a great virtual meeting, friends—and happy connecting!

Alyssa Teubner
North Dakota State University
Assistant Director of New Student Programs

Introduction

Please don't read this book in order. We created this compilation to serve as a just-in-time reference guide that you could turn to when you needed to increase engagement. Each chapter stands on its own, and you have the freedom to jump around. In fact, you'll get the most out of this book if you:

1. Start at the table of contents.

2. Find a topic you are most curious about.

3. Read only that chapter.

4. Put the book down and experiment with what you've learned.

If you rinse and repeat these four steps, this book and the accompanying videos will serve as your personal coach and mentor. They'll ensure that your events, conferences, classes, training sessions and meetings go off without a hitch.

After adapting to a remote work environment, online teaching, virtual training and distance learning during the pandemic, we all discovered some things we loved and some things we loathed.

Being able to switch back and forth from virtual to in-person environments can give us all more flexibility. When done well, it can be more inclusive. Moving forward, organizations that are great at both will rise to the top.

Will and I firmly believe that genuine connections, high engagement and fantastic collaboration are all still perfectly possible when remote.

Each chapter of the book is based on a video from our YouTube channel dedicated to helping leaders and educators make connection easy. If you don't feel like reading, take out your phone and scan the QR code to make the chapter come to life! You'll find the main channel page, where videos are neatly sorted by topic:

You may also notice that almost every chapter and video title is a question. That's because each one of the 200+ videos on our channel is a response to a question that a leader or educator has asked. For example, a participant once stuck around on Zoom after I finished leading a workshop on the "5 Ingredients for Virtual Engagement." After everybody else clicked "leave meeting," they whispered, *"OK, so this is amazing, but how do you engage somebody when attendance is mandatory?"* Two weeks later, we released a video tutorial answering that very question.

In fact, if you ever bump up against a really specific question not addressed in the book, Will and I welcome you to email it to us at hello@weand.me. You might even make it into the second edition of the book and a fresh video tutorial!

Video is such a personal format, right? It's just you and me having a conversation. To bring some of this humanity into each chapter, you'll find actual YouTube comments pasted at the start of the chapter. Sometimes there is a little dialogue and bonus tips or ideas. Other comments are simply there to invite you to feel connected to all the other leaders and educators seeking to make connection and engagement easy for their people.

Lastly, there are times throughout the book where I mention card decks we've created and other tools. While you are free to order those from our website, I believe information should be free, so we've made printable versions of them freely available at www.weand.me/free. We will continue updating this page with new and improved resources.

With gratitude,
Chad
We and Me
Co-founder and Chief Experience Officer
Speaker, Mentor, and Co-creator of the Connection Toolkit™

5

ESSENTIAL INGREDIENTS FOR ENGAGEMENT

Chapter 1 is based on this video!

We!

 Katherine   1 day ago

As an educator, I especially appreciate the notion that engagement is heightened when participants are contributors, not just consumers.

         REPLY

 Chad Littlefield   1 day ago

Designing for contribution is the single greatest impact you can have on engagement BEFORE a class, session, program, meeting, or virtual conference begins. Our brains are "wired to wander" when gatherings are designed only for sit-and-get style instruction. Glad to have you on the Connector team, Katherine 👍

      REPLY

 Katherine   1 day ago

Love this and the ideas you are sharing. We can look at gathering differently in terms of what makes remote better rather than what we are losing. These five ingredients offer a perfect framework. I look forward to more tips! Keep up the good work.

         REPLY

1

How Can Active Participation in Meetings Be Encouraged?

5 Ingredients for Success

This is one of the most valuable things I share with all of my clients, who are some of the top leaders and educators on the planet. A big chunk of my job is helping those leaders and educators make connection and engagement easy—both online and off. Below are five essential ingredients to do just that.

By the end of the chapter, I guarantee you'll be able to answer this question: How can active participation in meetings be encouraged?

You can think about these five ingredients as they occur throughout the meeting, from start to finish. But you don't always need to infuse all of these ingredients into every single meeting. In fact, I would recommend you don't, because it would be a lot. Instead, try to incorporate a couple of ingredients into each meeting. By doing that, I guarantee that you'll see active participation increase.

Also, I teach and share this in the context of virtual and remote meetings, but these ideas are just as relevant and important for in-person gatherings as well.

1. Unofficial Start

The first ingredient is the unofficial start. I got this term from Mark Collard, director of *playmeo* and an experiential trainer and consultant, who pointed out that we tend to reward people for being late. We wait a few minutes for people's Wi-Fi to catch up or for their commute (even if it's just from the kitchen to the home office).

The unofficial start says don't do that. That unofficial start should run from a few minutes before the official start time to a few minutes after the scheduled start to reward the people who showed up early, while also showing understanding for people who might be shuffling in a bit late. For a 9 a.m. meeting, have the unofficial start run from, say, 8:55 to 9:03.

> That unofficial start should run from a few minutes before the official start time to a few minutes after the scheduled start to reward the people who showed up early.

With this approach, you immediately and purposefully engage people. There are a lot of ways to do that. One of my favorite ways utilizes a deck of cards I created called We! Connect Cards. These are being used by universities and organizations all over the world to help create conversations that matter.

I might hold up a question like this one: "What are people usually surprised to find out about you?" or "What are you grateful for?" Then I ask people, just as they're joining the meeting, if they can jot down their answer on a sticky note and hold that up to a camera to share with the group virtually. If it's an in-person meeting, I might have them sit next to somebody they don't typically sit next to and start a conversation riffing off this question. That's immediately engaging. More often than not, I choose an unofficial start that helps me connect everyone to the purpose of the gathering as well.

2. Context Hook

The second ingredient is probably the most important ingredient to create active participation. Without it, you risk people being "present," but in totally different worlds. The context hook could be reduced to as little as one sentence or turned into a quick five-minute experience or illustration.

The purpose is to "hook" your attendees into the same context.

The first way I frame the context hook is by getting clear about what my intention is for the meeting and making sure that it's others-centric. I think about an intention like a rubber band that stretches over the needs of everyone in the meeting and pulls people together. By contrast, most of the time an "objective" is laser-focused. An agenda item is very task-focused—it's the thing that we need to get done, and it might not incorporate what other people care about or need.

In short, I'm going to get clear about my other-centered intention and state it in a way that resonates with the group, so I use their language, not mine. For example, I was leading a workshop on how to make virtual connection and engagement easy for 125 executives at a big national insurance company. I knew that some of them didn't want to be there, so my context hook was really important to grab everyone's attention.

To engage the group I essentially told them that "whether they wanted to be there or not, my intention was to be a painkiller for the next 100-plus hours they'd have to spend in meetings." For most of them, they were going to meet that mark in two or three weeks—as executives spend a lot of time in meetings. That was my other-centric approach.

Not many people love meetings. Given that, the idea that maybe this hour could actually make the next 100 hours of their meetings less exhausting and more productive got these executives curious. They played along because they wanted to know how they could make that happen.

That's the purpose of a context hook. Sometimes I use this ingredient to invite people to shift their state. A mentor of mine, Matt Church, likes to say that state matters more than script. This is a really valuable idea.

I do another exercise where I invite people to cover their camera on Zoom. If you're meeting in person, you can just have people turn around with their backs to the group. Then invite the group to get into a certain state of mind by sharing a quick narrative. For example, I might tell the group to imagine that they're in the most boring, terrible meeting they've ever attended. I'll have them picture the facial expressions they're making, and imagine their posture, and what they're thinking and feeling. Then, on the count of three, I'll have them remove that object in front of their camera (or turn around to face the group), and be in that state. They'll wear that facial expression and take on that posture. On Zoom in gallery view, it's awesome. The exercise puts everybody in this worst-meeting-ever state.

Of course, you shouldn't end there. That would be a bad context hook. For the second round, cover your cameras, and this time imagine traveling to a brand new city that you have never traveled to before. You're on a train, and it arrives at the station. There, one of your absolute best friends of all time is standing on the platform much to your surprise. Imagine your state, your facial expression, your gestures, and be in that state.

Use this opportunity to promote how your workshop will be way more interesting, engaging and energizing than the average webinar. That's a great way to hook people from the beginning.

3. Connection Before Content

I talk about this idea of putting connection before content in all of my work. My co-founder at We and Me, Will Wise, and I wrote a book about it called Ask Powerful Questions: Create Conversations That Matter.

Peter Block, who coined the phrase, claims that connection before content must have three ingredients.

It must:

1. Connect to the purpose–make it clear why people are there.
2. Connect people to each other.
3. Create choice and space for authenticity and vulnerability.

Typically, connection before content is going to involve breaking into small groups with two to five people talking about a question that connects to the purpose of why they're there and allows them to connect to each other. The best questions invite people to share a story or personal experience. Throughout this book, there are dozens of other methods and exercises to make connection before content happen as well.

> **The best questions invite people to share a story or personal experience.**

4. Content

The fourth ingredient is content. This usually makes up about 80% of most meetings or gatherings. You've got an agenda, with things to address and talk about. My tip for spurring active participation is to make your content as visual and experiential as possible. In other words, design your content for contribution—not consumption.

We remember visuals and experiential data much better than language and numbers alone, and the brain loves participating in and contributing to experiences. Yet if you rewind the tape, probably the last 10 meetings you attended were 90% language and numbers, which you're unlikely to remember.

5. Closing

The fifth ingredient is also the most often forgotten one. It is burned into my memory, though, since meeting a woman at an event, who introduced herself as a professional storyteller. I asked what her best tip was for telling really phenomenal stories. Without pause, she said, 'all you've got to do is know the first and last sentence you're going to say and you can kind of fill in the middle.'

Having a background in psychology, I found this fascinating because it aligned with the primacy/recency effect. This is where we tend to remember what happens first and last more than what happens in the middle. How you end your meetings is extremely important to setting the expectation for your team for the next meeting and affects how they'll take what they've learned and apply it to their work.

My facilitator/leader version of the storyteller's advice is to know the first experience you're going to start with and the last experience that you're going to end with for each meeting. In the same way, if you go into meetings knowing ahead of time which of these five ingredients you're going to include to engage your team, you're bound to increase participation.

THINK
DIFFERENTLY

Chapter 2 is based on this video!

The Extraordinary Zone   2 days ago

Most Zoom/online meetings bore me to tears and I abhor the "I'm just waiting a few minutes for everyone to jump on" line. For several years I have wished that sentence and action could be erased from every meeting. I am punctual and most times, early. Having some connection time before the official start of the meeting actually helps attendees become 'in tune' with timeliness especially if there are some nuggets that they have fear of missing out on. I believe that changing how we do online meetings is critical at this juncture in time. Thank you for the tips. Everyone of them hits the mark.

       REPLY

Chad Littlefield   2 days ago

Hey there, thanks so much for commenting! I love that YouTube allows us to be in dialogue as opposed to a purely one-way interaction! As a small thanks for connecting, here is a free sample of a new prototype "fill in the blank" style question deck we are currently working on: https://weand.me/2020/10/29/what-are-some-really-good-icebreaker-questions/

Happy connecting! Looking forward to seeing you in the comments section of other episodes 😊

     REPLY

2

What is it Like to Participate in a Virtual Meeting?

Navigating the Critics, Consumers and Contributors

People are usually surprised to find out that my job is helping others have better virtual gatherings. At least that's part of what I do. I've facilitated over 500 interactive remote meetings, webinars and interactive keynotes—interactive being the key word here. And I love it! I exist on the planet to make connection and engagement easy both online and offline.

Altogether, I've spent the equivalent of several months of life in virtual meetings. So I have a sense of what they're like. You probably do as well, given our pandemic experience of working remotely. But it's important to truly understand the nuances of coming together online in order to design engaging and impactful virtual meetings.

To start, there's a lot of variation in the experience. To illustrate that, I want to put you in the shoes of a couple of people I've seen in my virtual workshops and sessions.

I frequently lead a workshop titled 'How to Make Virtual Engagement Easy.' In one of those online sessions, a woman was sitting in a chair when a child appeared in the background. Her 8-year-old son, who was barely perceptible at first, snuck up closer until he disappeared right behind her. Then he pops his arms out on either side of her and starts waving them up and down. His mom, who paid a good bit for this workshop, is oblivious.

Taking it all in you can't help but be reminded that virtual meetings can be, among other things, chaotic. Commonly, when you join virtual meetings you're in your own home. There are family members screaming about spaghetti, FedEx delivery people ringing your doorbell and dogs barking. At least sometimes it feels like that. At other times, virtual sessions can be really quiet—dead quiet actually. The vacuum of mute can contribute to an odd sense of isolation despite being live with a group.

My brother-in-law was taking some online classes, and when he was visiting, he needed to log into a class. I found him downstairs on his laptop. He looked up and gave me this kind of knowing head nod—like, "I'm in class." So I ate lunch nearby without saying a word. Do you know what it was like for him to be "in" that virtual meeting? Totally silent. Pure consumption. Not a peep from the student.

Those two experiences speak to the variation in virtual meetings. But it goes beyond that. People also have different mindsets when they come together online, which usually fall into three buckets. These are not types of people. We're talking about states of mind, not traits. They may sound like traits, but we oscillate between these on a moment-to-moment basis.

By understanding the different mindsets, you'll be empowered to create better virtual meetings. So here's how it breaks down.

The Critics

Sometimes people are really comfortable pointing out what's wrong in the world, but they're totally uninterested in doing anything about it. These are your critics. They might have their arms crossed—literally—or have a closed mindset.

Your critics are thinking the meeting should have been an email, and they can't wait for it to be over.

The Consumers

Next, you have those who might absorb everything but passively. They're not really chiming in. They're kind of just there and they don't get involved. These are your consumers.

In the same way that you and I might mindlessly scroll through our favorite social media app, consumers are taking in the world around them, but they aren't "posting" too much.

The Contributors

Finally, you have another group that does get involved. They're not victims to their own experience or the agenda their boss has set out. They're contributors. They're here to actively add to and shape their world.

The world needs more folks in this state of mind. You want people with this mindset on your team. They make your job as a leader or educator easier and more impactful.

Design Your Meetings for Contribution

Obviously, if you're leading or attending a virtual meeting, you want more contributors and fewer critics and consumers. The thing is, we can't make anybody be anything. What we can do, however, is design our meetings for active contribution, not consumption.

To get hyper-specific, I would say you want this kind of meaningful, purposeful contribution, on average, about every seven minutes. That means going beyond asking, "Hey, what do you think about this?"

> You want this kind of meaningful, purposeful contribution, on average, about every seven minutes...

Truly check in with people. Have them rate the meeting on a scale of 1 to 10, where 10 is essentially the best meeting they've ever been in, and 1 is "you should have just sent this in an email."

You can even have the group hold up that many fingers to the camera as a quick, fun visual to take the group's temperature. If people have video off, you can ask the same question in chat and have team members respond there. If people aren't a 10, ask, "What can we do to make this a 10 out of 10 for you?"

You're in a Bad Movie

I think that participating in a virtual meeting is kind of like watching a really crappy home video that was filmed on the original iPhone. That's basically what a video call is. It's poorly orchestrated. It's not particularly interesting. There's not a lot of good conflict or active engagement. There are no explosions or crazy car chase scenes. It's a pretty lousy movie that feels like it happens in slow motion, and it's really pixelated. There can be a lag when we're online that slows or temporarily stops conversations and leaves people who are speaking in the lurch.

One of the things I like to do to give people a better experience in virtual meetings is let them know what to expect in advance. To do this, I'll record a video using a tool like Loom or VidYard that sets out the intention for the meeting. (You can find these at Loom. com or VidYard.com).

I get people excited by talking about what's in it for them. I set expectations and might encourage people to show up "video ready" if they're able. And since I'll be asking for everyone to share their perspective throughout the session, I may invite them to have their keyboard ready and fingers warmed up to share in chat.

Sending a video like that beforehand is really helpful. That's especially true if you're leading a webinar or some kind of facilitated training and people don't know what to expect. In a larger virtual event or webinar, I've noticed a simple video beforehand increases both attendance and engagement significantly. One virtual experience can be totally different than the next. You might be in a highly interactive virtual meeting where everyone has something to say. Or you could be attending an online college class that's designed for consumption, rather than contribution, with only the professor speaking.

Given the range, you've got to set expectations about the kind of experience you're trying to create before people actually show up. What you don't want is for people to be surprised when they log into a meeting. It would stink to join a virtual meeting right after you just went for a five-mile run only to realize that you need to have your video on. With an existing team, having a simple discussion about what the virtual norms and agreements are can alleviate many future headaches and issues.

> With an existing team, having a simple discussion about what the virtual norms and agreements are can alleviate many future headaches and issues.

If you're looking for ways to make virtual meetings better, that's what I do. Will Wise and I created the *Connection Toolkit* to make it easy for leaders and educators to amplify connection, belonging and trust. You can purchase the toolkit so you have it on hand for meetings, or get all our free resources at:

> www.weand.me/free

There are more than 100 group exercises, which work for groups of all sizes. You can use questions from the deck of *We! Connect Cards* to create conversations that matter. It's a really great way to start meetings with connection before content and to make your virtual gatherings more active and engaged.

Chapter 3 is based on this video!

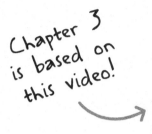 

 Jackie 3 days ago

Thank you for the much-needed positivity around virtual meetings!

    REPLY

 Chad Littlefield 3 days ago

There is definitely a little bit of "womp, womp, womp" developing for some people around virtual meetings. Being intentional about meeting differently, adding structure, and making time for creative connections can make a measurable difference in meeting more meaningfully online.

   REPLY

3

How are Virtual Meetings Different from Face-To-Face Meetings?

7 Differences—and 1 Key Similarity

With awareness of key differences and similarities, we can design better meetings. My job is working with some of the most intelligent and innovative companies and universities to help make connection and engagement easy. When that happens, meetings and events come alive. But to do this, we must first understand how virtual and face-to-face meetings are different.

Both have their advantages and disadvantages. So whether you meet online or in-person, where you compare the two, it's kind of like teleportation gone wrong. You lose some things—like you might end up missing a limb. But you gain others, like arriving to find you have an extra finger. In reality, each offers something that the other doesn't.

It's important as well to recognize that there's one overriding similarity whether you're meeting face-to-face or online. This is something we can harness to make our meetings more engaging, impactful and effective. But before we get to that similarity, let's first cover the seven ways meeting virtually and in person is different.

What's Different

1. **In virtual meetings, we only see heads.**

   Unlike in-person meetings, there is far less shared context in virtual meetings. Online, we are just talking (or silent) heads, give or take our shoulders and hands coming into the frame on occasion. Sure, that's a playful difference. But it speaks to the fact that you have a whole lot less shared context to start with in virtual meetings.

2. **When you meet in person, you have more nonverbal clues and insight.**

   There's a whole lot less nonverbal context while remote. You can't see how everyone is reacting to what you're discussing. You miss the smiles and the eye rolls.

   On the other hand, research done at Stanford University's Virtual Human Interaction Lab found that we are getting eye contact and "face time" in overdrive in a virtual environ-ment. We are used to having more to look at than somebody's nose hairs.

3. **In virtual meetings, participants can mute themselves.**

   That's not really an option for an in-person meeting. When others are on mute, you miss all the context. If you're sharing something as a leader, the meeting facilitator or a trainer, you can't hear the chuckles or the side conversations. Whether others are on mute or unmuted makes a big difference.

4. **When you meet virtually, you have a fridge.**

   That allows you to procrastinate and eat lots of food when you don't want to do work. When you meet in person, you're kind of trapped and present. You have no fridge. We have to acknowledge that we have distractions at home. Accordingly, we've got to be intentional about how we carve out space and time to be present.

That's not to say working remotely doesn't have its advantages. Maybe you get to have lunch with your kids or your spouse, or your dog or, say, your lizard.

5. Working at home, you can use your world to connect.

When you're virtual, you are surrounded by everything in your world. You have a different kind of personal context that you don't have when you're in an office or meet in person.

In a face-to-face meeting, I can't ask you to grab an object that represents a part of who you are. Right now, since I'm at home, I can quickly grab a picture of Otto, my son, who was born not so long ago on Jan. 1, 2020. I couldn't do that quite as easily if we met in a conference room.

> When we meet virtually while working from home, there are lots of creative ways we can use people's spaces.

When we meet virtually while working from home, there are lots of creative ways we can use people's spaces. Invite people to leave their virtual bubble to go grab something that represents a topic they want to share or their takeaway from the meeting. Incorporating these kinds of analog visuals, and inviting movement and activity, can increase meeting engagement. The rest of this book is piled high with ideas to do just that!

With face-to-face meetings, you're stuck with what you have, or what you bring to the meeting. If you're in an office or classroom, all you have to work with is what's in that space. I think this is why some people describe their workplace environment as a bit stale.

6. In person, we have organic connection.

When we meet in-person, people show up a couple minutes early. We have side conversations. An organization's culture develops at the water cooler.

Virtually, we're in a vacuum until whenever the meeting starts. Then we click the link and we pop into our little portal. We lose that organic connection. But we can be more intentional about how we connect.

I think and write a lot about connection. That's why I created the *We! Connection Toolkit*. It's designed to amplify connection, belonging and trust with a whole heap of activities and novel group exercises.

I know how important connection is. A mountain of research says if we don't connect, engagement, morale and productivity all go way down. So when we're working and meeting remotely, it's really important to build in time for that connection before we jump into content.

But we also need to be intentional about how we connect. We can't just rely on the idle chit-chat and small talk that some people, especially introverts, dread. Instead, start off the meeting with more meaningful, intentional prompts, questions or exercises.

7. Virtually, it's easy to use visuals.

Consider starting your meeting with an idea or quote. We have one quote in the *We! Connection Toolkit*, for example, from Alan Alda: "Listening is being able to be changed by the other person."

I can share that really easily just by holding up the card with the quote. And you can do the same. Then ask what everyone thinks of that quote or idea.

In person, visuals often require more work. I need to print handouts or write something on a whiteboard.

But virtually, we can easily use analog visuals to make our content come alive. This method is almost like magic because you can make anything outside the range of your camera simply appear in the blink of an eye. When used well, this approach can be extremely engaging for attendees.

A Key Similarity

For all the ways virtual and face-to-face meetings differ, there's one really important similarity: the purpose. This is the reason we're coming together, and it's the same whether we're online or in the same room.

I think we do ourselves a disservice when we let logistical concerns trip us up. We can spend too much time and energy trying to convert face-to-face meetings into virtual ones. We should instead ask ourselves how we can creatively accomplish our purpose. What can we do even better virtually?

That means using the space around us and the access people have to the internet. The entire world of information is a single click away when you're on a video call. Also, use the chat. When you're meeting virtually, everyone can speak and listen to each other at the exact same time in the chat.

> For all the ways virtual and face-to-face meetings differ, there's one really important similarity: the purpose.

At the beginning of a meeting, everyone can introduce themselves in under 30 seconds using chat. In person, that might take 15 or 20 minutes to get around the room. When we're introducing ourselves one at a time, we're focused on ourselves. It's very hard to actually hear anybody around us. When we're meeting virtually, everyone can quickly type their intro into the chat. Then they can scroll up the chat and focus on the group. We can flip that perspective from me, me, me to a focus on others. You can actually accelerate your purpose and conversations online, although it does take a bit of additional structure or facilitation.

Brainstorming 101 is to come up with ideas alone first and together second. Virtually you can have everyone type their idea for a particular project or task into the chat without pressing enter. Then have everyone press enter to share their ideas at the same time. This is a great way to avoid groupthink.

That's much harder to do in person. You've got to get sticky notes, which can get messy. Then you have to think about how you're going to capture the ideas that are jotted down on the sticky notes.

Ultimately, there are a lot of advantages and disadvantages to meeting both virtually and in person. You can't replace that context or shared experience you have when you meet face to face.

It's better then, as Priya Parker's suggests in The Art of Gathering: How We Meet and Why It Matters, to focus instead on meeting for purpose rather than time. Think about why you're meeting. Then consider how you can use the tools and the differences we discussed to make your meeting come alive and accomplish your goals.

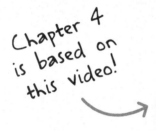

Chapter 4 is based on this video!

Lisa 4 days ago

I've been watching videos and webinars on this topic for weeks, looking for ideas for improving my consulting and training business. You are hands down THE BEST. Thank you for your engaging and incredibly useful material, Chad. Today you improved on an already amazing library of excellent videos!

   REPLY

— 4 —

A Virtual Meeting
is the Same Thing As...

3 Useful Metaphors that Will
Help You Design Better
Virtual Experiences

Because my job involves helping others make virtual engagement and connection really easy, I am often asked an elemental question: What are virtual meetings like?

To find answers, I typed a simple query into Google: "a virtual meeting is the same thing as ..." and let search suggestions fill in the blank. The dropdown list finished my sentence, alternatively, with "a humidifier," "a ticket" and "a pressure cooker."

Reframing the Virtual Meeting: Think of It Like...

Inspired by what I found, I'd like to give you three new lenses to view virtual meetings through for a fresh perspective, so that you can make them more productive, impactful and effective. You can use these metaphors to reframe virtual meetings for yourself and others.

Here's what these three metaphors could mean for your virtual gatherings.

A Humidifier

I wanted to learn more about the first term my search returned. So I asked Google, What does a humidifier do? Well, according to MayoClinic.org, humidifiers ease problems caused by dry air. Based on that alone, I would say a great virtual meeting is like a humidifier in the sense that it infuses something into the air to make problems go away. Really, any good meeting should do this.

In her book, *The Art of Gathering*, Priya Parker talks about the value of meeting for purpose rather than for time. Yet often, we don't meet with a purpose or problem-solving intention, and instead come together merely because we have a meeting on our calendar.

To go back to the humidifier, what it does—putting it in unscientific terms—is essentially inject water into the air to make it a bit more breathable. I would say really great virtual meetings actually inject a number of things into a group dynamic that help ease problems in that group.

> Really great virtual meetings actually inject a number of things into a group dynamic that help ease problems in that group.

So I want you to think about virtual meetings through this lens, and ask yourself the question, "What can I infuse into my team in this meeting?" Then consider how you can invite your team to crowdsource that infusion. As the leader, you're not solely responsible for bringing positive things to the group dynamic. You can ask for them, too.

On any virtual meeting platform, you can invite people to quickly share in the chat one thing they really want to accomplish by the end of the meeting. Once everyone types their responses, you'll essentially have an instant written agenda. By comparison, at an in-person meeting, it might take 20 minutes to go around the room while everybody shares their piece.

A Ticket

To really simplify this, let's start with the obvious. Tickets suck—at least that's true for traffic tickets, like when you get pulled over for speeding—and sometimes virtual meetings suck, too.

Human beings are not made to be confined to a three-foot wide box and glued to a screen. We have the world's most amazing autofocus device—two of them in fact—our eyes. Yet what do we do with that capacity? We spend our days staring at a screen that's 20 inches away from our faces.

All that to say, virtual meetings are not the same as meeting in person. You have limited context and some aspects of virtual meetings just kind of stink. When everybody is on mute, and something funny happens, you can see everybody laughing, but you don't actually hear it. That vacuum of digital silence takes something away from the humanity of the experience.

But to take the ticket analogy a little further, I would say there's a benefit to tickets (and the traffic laws they enforce). It might be hard to appreciate this if you're the one getting fined. But the threat of getting a ticket prevents people from driving 120 miles per hour on the highway and recklessly endangering others on the road.

In the same way, there are also benefits to virtual meetings.

Like a ticket, these meetings help create structure, and without that, we'd have chaos.

There are also some huge upsides. As leaders and educators, you get to choose which angle you emphasize. I wrote this book because there are things that we can do virtually that we can't do in person. There are things we can actually do better virtually. Each chapter is filled with tools and examples meant for you to ruthlessly reinterpret and apply to your own context.

> Like a ticket, these meetings help create structure, and without that, we'd have chaos.

Think about brainstorming. It takes a lot of effort to avoid groupthink when you're meeting in person. That's because we usually honor the extroverts—they talk first— and we don't give people time to really think and process information.

When you're meeting virtually, you can invite people to shut off their cameras. Then you can ask everyone to write down five ideas for solving a problem, putting each idea on a different sticky note. Over five rounds, you can have each person hold up one sticky note at a time to their camera. If you have three people in a meeting, you can share 15 ideas in a span of less than five minutes with this method.

Now compare that to trying to come up with 15 ideas during an in-person meeting, which could take an hour. That's just one example of how we can creatively use the remote meeting format to our advantage.

A Pressure Cooker

If I think about a pressure cooker, I want to take out whatever I'm preparing at the right time. Maybe I put a pork loin with some sauce, onions and spices into the sealed pot, which uses steam pressure to cook. I want the meat to be totally tender, but I don't want it to completely dissolve or fall apart.

Thinking about this from a hosting perspective, it's always best to end a party while it's still fun. I would say this applies to virtual meetings as well. If you're noticing that people appear to be a little burnt out in a meeting, you should have wrapped up 10 minutes ago.

Now there are times when you might need to meet for a longer period of time. But if you do, make sure to incorporate regular breaks to turn off your camera and check in with yourself. Think about what your brain and body need, and encourage others to do the same. Take a stretch break and come back refreshed.

Don't just take the kind of "break" that's really code for catching up on email and returning to the meeting as quickly as possible. That doesn't actually help us to be refreshed and offset Zoom fatigue. Remembering the pressure cooker, make sure to take breaks *before* people are exhausted.

As you approach your next virtual meeting, try to think of it as being like a humidifier, a ticket and a pressure cooker. These three questions summarize the mindset and momentum each of these metaphors can help create.

1. A Humidifier: What can I infuse into my group?
2. A Ticket: How can I focus on the bright spots of this pixelated world?
3. A Pressure Cooker: How can I end the party while it is still fun?

Looking at virtual meetings through these three lenses can make connection and engagement easier online as you meet, work and collaborate remotely.

Chapter 5 is based on this video!

 Heather   3 weeks ago

I'm continuing to work remotely while my five colleagues are back in the office. I try to connect with them by phone and quick Zoom touch-base meetings but I struggle with this. Any ideas on how to make staying connected more fun? I'm trying to mirror the hallway and "water cooler" conversations but there's no specific agenda.

          REPLY

 Chad Littlefield   3 weeks ago

SUPER valuable question, Heather. First of all, I'd strongly recommend establishing a purpose for these conversations. The idea of "unofficial starts and ends" in this video may also be useful: https://youtu.be/Oz27RB09Rd8   Finally, because you are remote, but others are not, just suggesting that you kick off at least some meetings with some "connection before content" where you actually bring the prompt/question/idea and invite folks to share could be powerful. ESPECIALLY, if you state that your intent is to replace the organic connection you miss out on.

 Heather   2 weeks ago

Thanks! BTW ... I love your "How to Make Online Meetings More Engaging" video! I have shared it with everyone I know. I found it especially useful for a teen group that has shifted to doing everything by Zoom. These young leaders learned a lot and they are running much better, and engaged, meetings now. Thank you for your work!

5

How to Overcome the Challenges of Virtual Teams

Use this Data to Problem-Solve and Realize the Benefits of Remote Work

No doubt you've encountered your share of obstacles operating as a virtual team. Data collected on remote workers helps us better understand the challenges they face and the benefits of virtual work. After we cover both, I'll share a couple clever strategies I've used to help teams overcome struggles associated with remote work.

Remote Struggles

Even pre-pandemic, the social media management platform Buffer was one of the most highly regarded all-remote teams. The company has been hiring remote workers since 2011, and it got rid of its office in 2015. It's been transparent about what works and what doesn't.

Each year, the company has put out its "State of Remote Work Report," asking thousands of workers about the challenges and benefits of remote work. In Buffer's 2020 report, 20% of surveyed employees named collaboration and communication as their most significant challenge. The same percentage said loneliness was their biggest struggle.

It can be wonderful to work from home. It can also be very isolating. Research has found that people who are socially integrated tend to live longer. It's not just about deep relationships. Generally feeling connected to your community (even recognizing the mail carrier and seeing the same people each time you go to the gym), and having friends to talk to can make all the difference.

> **Research has found that people who are socially integrated tend to live longer.**

When you're working from home, you can be deeply embedded in your family, and at the same time, disconnected from people in your organization. Remote workers who live alone can feel all the more isolated.

On the other hand, some people feel like they can't break away from the virtual workplace. Eighteen percent of the remote employees Buffer surveyed said not being able to unplug was the most significant challenge they faced. Twelve percent struggled most with distractions at home.

Another 10% found it difficult to be in a different time zone than teammates. That's why you need to be careful about hiring employees who live in extremely incompatible time zones when the job requires much synchronous communication and connection.

Say you need to spend a lot of time on Slack or Zoom. Well, you're not going to get the best out of your team if someone needs to wake up at 2 a.m. to meet virtually with another member of the team on the other side of the world else at 3 p.m. Being deliberate in your hiring can help you avoid these kinds of time zone issues.

For companies that need to hire across multiple time zones, preparation and planning are key. If people are flexible so that it's possible to create at least a two- to three-hour schedule overlap every single day for distant team members, that can make a big difference.

Now that's just one very specific concern. Your group's struggles might be a little different. But where you face similar challenges, as I expect you might, please feel free to steal and adapt anything I mention to apply it to your context.

Also, as you look for solutions, it's important to consider the biggest benefits of working remotely. In their book, *Switch: How to Change Things When Change Is Hard*, Chip and Dan Heath talk about this idea of finding the "bright spot." If you're trying to overcome struggles, you don't want to necessarily put all your focus on those challenges. Instead, also pay attention to what's working well.

Buffer found that 32% of employees surveyed see being able to have a flexible schedule as the biggest benefit of working remotely. In addition, 26% liked having the flexibility to work from anywhere most of all. And 21% said not having to commute was the biggest benefit.

Flexibility was a theme that emerged time and again.

Then there was this question: "Would you like to work remotely, at least some of the time, for the rest of your career?" Almost everyone—a whopping 98%—answered yes to that. We still don't know exactly how the pandemic will affect attitudes toward remote work, but this is something most of us want to do at least some of the time.

Finding the Bright Spot

It can be easy to focus on the struggles. But it's very beneficial to look for bright spots. Check in with your remote team to determine what's working well, and then dissect that.

By doing this, you can find bright spots within challenges. Say, for example, you've heard from your team that they're really struggling with feeling isolated and disconnected from the rest of the world. Ask if there was a time in the last month where they really felt connected to the team or their community. You could set aside 20 to 30 minutes each week to talk about what's been working to improve collaboration and communication.

In this way you can ask questions to look for the bright spots. This is different from saying, 'Hey, I know everybody's struggling with loneliness and isolation, how are you doing with that?' It's fine to check in like that. But with this strategy, by identifying the bright spot and dissecting it, you can learn how to replicate it in the future. That allows you to go beyond focusing on the problem to create a lasting solution.

Psychologist Barbara Fredrickson describes this type of orientation with her "broaden-and-build theory of positive emotions." When we fixate on our struggles, it can narrow our thinking. By contrast, according to the broaden-and-build theory, positive emotions contribute to resilience and well-being, and broaden our awareness. This can help us to come up with novel approaches to tackle the challenges we face.

Making Flexibility Your Solution

The biggest benefit of working remotely, flexibility, can also be used as a tool to overcome challenges.

If everyone is feeling isolated or disconnected, for example, you could stop work at 3 p.m. on a given day each week. Then alternate what you do with that time at the end of the day. Set aside that window from 3 p.m. to 5 p.m., say on a Friday, for employees to connect on even weeks. Then on odd weeks allow people to cut out of work early to spend time with family and friends.

> The biggest benefit of working remotely, flexibility, can also be used as a tool to overcome challenges.

Meet briefly to brainstorm other ways to create meaningful connections. The focused strategy of finding the bright spot and then using flexibility as a tool to problem-solve can be instrumental in overcoming the challenges virtual teams face.

If you're looking for more resources to help your team connect, you can pick up a *Connection Toolkit*. Have the kit shipped to your home or access a free downloadable version at www.weand.me/free. We created this toolkit to help teams amplify connection, belonging and trust. There are a ton of group exercises for teams of all sizes that allow you to do that, no matter what challenges your remote team faces.

GET STARTED

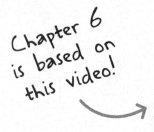

Chapter 6 is based on this video!

We!

James 1 month ago

You are speaking my language. I have found this 'virtual' world of the last six months to be painful, boring and unproductive 85% of the time. Why? Lack of skill or planning by the host to be intentional about the meeting/event being productive, engaging and connecting. Those of us who show up early, or on time, feel like we have waded into the 'wasted time' zone. And, if I hear another person say 'I'm just going to wait a few seconds (minutes) to see who pops on,' I think I will choke on my coffee. I am giving you thumbs up, thumbs up, thumbs up. Thank you!

     REPLY

6

How to Create an Agenda for a Virtual Meeting

Set Your Intentions in Real Time and Get Your Team Involved

Recently, I led a virtual team meeting and afterward, about 20% of the team emailed me asking to see a picture of my floor. The reason? Well, that has everything to do with how you can create an agenda for a virtual team meeting.

I'm going to unpack the technique I use, which I think you'll really love. Whether you have a large or small group, it will make your meetings immediately more interesting, engaging and memorable.

Then for those of you who have too much to do and too little time, I'll share a second technique to set an agenda *while* you're meeting virtually. You can do this with zero prep time at the beginning of the meeting.

All the Buzz About My Floor

The reason so many people were curious about my floor was because that's where I had laid out my agenda. If I want my agenda for a virtual meeting to be more engaging and interesting, I create an analog version. I don't put it on a PowerPoint slide or a digital word document.

In this case, I had my agenda stretched out as a series of 10 to 15 objects on the floor. I knew the meeting was going to take place in the order I had it laid out. So when we finished object No. 1, we moved to object No. 2.

> If I want my agenda for a virtual meeting to be more engaging and interesting, I create an analog version.

First, I had a question that I held up to the camera and invited people to answer in the chat. Then, I put on a hat that helped me visually frame the intention for the session. Then I held up an object that represented a story to kick things off, and on it went.

There's also an entire design framework that I had in mind when I created the agenda and flow for the session. I incorporated ingredients we talked about in the first chapter that make virtual engagement easy. That includes hooking people on the reason for the meeting by clearly stating your intention and engaging team members right away during the unofficial start.

For other meetings and even when I record video tutorials, I might have a simple agenda laid out on my desk. At the beginning of the virtual meeting, I sometimes hold up a quote. I have one from Norah Jones in front of me right now: "I don't try to sound like anyone but me anymore," she says. "If something is out of my element, I try to avoid it." With the right group, that may be a powerful way to frame the context or purpose of a gathering.

I would simply hold up a card with the quote on it to show the group as an unofficial start to the meeting. I do this while people are logging in and before I've gotten to any official agenda items. I might just invite people to unmute or type in the chat what this quote makes them think about.

The unofficial start gets things rolling. It sparks some immediate engagement. It's not obligatory small talk—like, How was your weekend? What's new? That doesn't really energize a meeting in any way. Kicking off with something that is both novel and thoughtfully connected to the purpose of the gathering sparks great energy at the beginning of a meeting.

You could choose a quote, question, activity or prompt that would fit the purpose of your meeting. You don't need to spend more than a minute or two preparing for this.

Use Analog Visuals to Elaborate on Your Agenda

I like to use analog visuals during virtual meetings. So to set the tone for a meeting and check the temperature, I might use two oversized cardboard emojis: an overwhelmed, sad face and a thumbs up. Then I'll tell everyone, if you're feeling a little bit overwhelmed, exhausted and unclear about what you're doing this month (holding up the overwhelmed emoji), my hope is that you leave feeling like, "Aha, I got it" (thumbs up) by meeting's end.

When I hold these visual elements up to the webcam, something in people's brains goes off. Most agendas are just an

81/2-by-11-inch document or a screen-shared PowerPoint slide. There's nothing really inherently wrong with those mediums. It's just that the brain loves visual data. So in a virtual meeting, it's really useful to mix it up. Do something interesting.

One of my favorite books, *Made to Stick: Why Some Ideas Survive and Others Die,* by Chip and Dan Heath, highlights the value of creating "curiosity gaps." This concept helps explain why so many people emailed me about my floor. You can see all this context behind me when I have my video on. But just out of frame in the "gap" was my agenda, all spread out. People wanted to see that visual element that was just out of sight.

Your agenda is the big picture snapshot of what you're going to do in your meeting. But you can also hold up analog visuals throughout the meeting to improve engagement.

After a while, people anticipate you're going to share more visuals. This creates what in psychology is described as variable reward. It's like when you pull that slot machine handle, you *could* always win. People wonder, "What's he going to hold up next?"

So if I tell the group we're going to start the meeting with a listening exercise, I might hold up a plushy ear. (Yes, I have one of those lying around for just such an occasion.) People seem to respond to that. It's like their brain says, "I'm awake, and I'm interested." All of a sudden this feels a little bit more real and purposeful.

Now I recognize this is a very unconventional way to set an agenda. It's also not practical to do all the time. You don't need to be going on a scavenger hunt around your house or your office and grabbing objects that fit your agenda for every single meeting.

But for a big meeting or when you really want to create a memorable experience, it may be worthwhile to prepare in this way.

Live Set Your Agenda During Your Virtual Meeting

The second technique I want to share is a really great tool to set a virtual meeting agenda in real time. A client I was working with calls it a "super chat."

You can do this on any virtual platform that has the chat feature. To execute a super chat, have everybody type something in the chat, and pause. Don't share it *yet*. Then, on the count of three, have everyone hit enter. All those chat messages will go through at the same time.

Should I be presenting to a big group, I might suggest that if we all press enter at the same time we could break Zoom or whatever platform we're using. Issuing a challenge like this just adds a pinch of intrigue.

A super chat is a phenomenal way to get your whole group involved and live set an agenda. The approach doesn't favor the extroverts and the leaders in the group, who would likely weigh in anyway. It encourages everyone to share their thoughts.

For a prompt I may ask, "What do you need to accomplish by the end of this 60 minutes to be able to feel like this was time well spent?" Then I'll have everyone type their answers into chat, but not hit enter immediately.

The result? You eliminate groupthink and everyone shares their outcome-focused intention for the meeting. The chat then serves as a reference point. It becomes the meeting agenda. Everyone has ownership of the meeting because they've all shared what they want to accomplish.

If people can't answer that prompt—or something like it—they probably shouldn't be in that meeting. Everyone should know why they're meeting or what they want to get out of the meeting.

As Priya Parker says, and I've repeated many times, we've got to meet for purpose, not for time. So often we set a meeting for a certain time. Then, whether there's an agenda or not, we meet for a set amount of time. Instead, we should know what we want to discuss and accomplish.

> We've got to meet for purpose, not for time.

Whatever it is, that needs to be laid out on the table in the very beginning. If you want to be a really great meeting facilitator, combine the two techniques above. Find out what people want to get accomplished at the beginning of the meeting. Then use analog visuals as prompts throughout the meeting. Doing that will greatly improve productivity, connection and engagement when you meet virtually.

Chapter 7 is based on this video!

Becca 4 hours ago

I love this. It was super helpful planning for an upcoming activist meeting!! You have such a spirit of play. Hoping to make our remote meetings a playful/productive ritual that we're all sharing in, instead of just another boring adult obligation. Thank you!

One quick question: If you're hosting and have to talk for an extended period, where do you aim your gaze on your camera? Like do you look straight into the camera, or a little below it?

      REPLY

 Chad Littlefield 2 hours ago

Think of your camera as the "friend of your best friend." So look at it fairly frequently, but it is fine to look at participants as well. Definitely recommend hiding self view though, so you don't need to look at yourself.

    REPLY

7

How to Run a Successful Virtual Meeting

Increase Engagement from the Unofficial Start to the Purposeful End of Your Session

This chapter is based on my 50th video tutorial focusing on how to make virtual engagement and connection easy for leaders and educators. By the end, you should have a whole mountain of strategies for running a successful virtual meeting.

Recently, I led a very fun virtual kickoff connection session at the Global Youth Entrepreneurship Festival. What I want to do is walk you through what that virtual conference session was like. That way you can ruthlessly reinterpret and steal all the tips, ideas and strategies that made this session so successful. We're going to focus particularly on back-end facilitator strategies. These are the strategies you as a leader or educator will want to keep in mind to run a successful virtual meeting.

In the connection lab at the Global Youth Entrepreneurship Festival, I wanted to first understand what the group knew really well. I explored this during our unofficial start to the session. The unofficial start is one of my favorite ideas or concepts. As I discuss in other chapters, this begins a few minutes before the scheduled start of a meeting, and is a way to engage people before a meeting officially gets underway. It continues a little bit after the official start to respect people who might show up late because of Wi-Fi issues, hungry kids, barking dogs or other remote obstacles.

The unofficial start is a brilliant way to kick off a session, and the easiest way to execute it is by asking a question. Check out the first chapter of the book for even more depth on the idea. I picked up the concept from a brilliant facilitator in Melbourne named Mark Collard. He's the founder of playmeo.com, the world's largest database of interactive, collaborative group activities.

> The unofficial start is a brilliant way to kick off a session, and the easiest way to execute it is by asking a question.

When I'm working with a group, my perspective is always that the group is collectively far smarter than I am. On this call, there were 150-plus people from all around the world. We had a lot of brain power at our disposal—about 450 pounds of brain actually, considering each adult brain weighs around three pounds. To access everyone's expertise, I love starting off with a question like: What is something you know really well? In this case, I added a little to the question: What is something you know really well that's *not* related to your work?

There's value in seeing how people answer questions like this. Your team members can share their answers in chat and connect with each other as they read the responses.

If you've read any other chapters or watched my YouTube tutorials, you know that I'm a huge believer in the power of having participants connect before jumping right into a meeting's agenda. I would argue that this is even more important virtually because of how much organic connection we lose when we don't meet in person. We don't get the informal time before a meeting begins. That's why we have to be intentional about creating that connection before content.

You can use virtual backgrounds and analog visuals to connect with your group. For the Virtual Connection Lab, I put on my son Otto's hat, and I encouraged others to wear my 1-year-old's hat as well. I put up a virtual background with a photo of Otto, wearing the exact same hat I had on—although, with his giant, toothless smile, he won a lot more points with the group than I did.

The photo of Otto that I shared was taken just a couple seconds after I showed him a plastic potato. It was from this little kitchen set we had. That giant, toothless grin was sparked by...a plastic potato! I told the group I wanted them to wear his hat so they could experience the kind of joy and love he had for learning.

The second hat I invited people to wear was a pirate hat, using a Zoom filter. This went with another theme: my encouragement to the group to "ruthlessly steal and reinterpret everything I said and did, and apply it to your own context." I find that phrase to be really useful, since each person knows best what their needs are for their work.

An Aside on Group Size
Make sure to keep group size in mind when you do a breakout at your next meeting. I used to work with a creativity and

innovation researcher at Penn State University, Dr. Sam Hunter. One of the things that he found was that the ideal group size for a creative brainstorming conversation is between four and seven people.

For breakouts on any digital platform, if you have three people or less, this could be a challenge. Not only is there not enough diversity of perspectives, but somebody's mic might be broken. Then you're down to a pair. If two people are having tech issues, forget it. You'll be down to one person meditating by themselves, frustrated that they can't talk to everybody else. Having four to seven people is ideal for breakouts, and I usually stick to four or five people per small group.

3 Quick Tips for Sparking Virtual Connection

Now, let's just do a lightning round. Here are three quick tips for sparking virtual connection in your organization.

1. Share highlights with each other.

There's so much value in sharing what is working well. That's especially true if there's a lot of change going on in the organization.

2. Use "teleporting" as a virtual concept.

I love talking about this idea. When we click a video conference link, we are teleporting to a completely new world. We're transported virtually along with everyone else who's meeting, and there's something really cool about having the ability to do that.

However, I would argue that teleporting actually takes a little bit longer than clicking a link to join a meeting. I've estimated that *true* teleportation takes about 60 seconds. We need a moment to connect with others and be present. To accommodate that, I'd suggest starting your meetings with 60 seconds of total silence like Will Wise and I usually do.

We shut off our videos, and we're just present. We don't do anything. We don't check our email. We don't swipe some feed. We do absolutely nothing, and let our minds wander.

It's amazing how, in that minute, your brain catches up to your body. Your body may have teleported virtually to another meeting, but your brain is still in the last meeting. It's still in the argument that you just had with your daughter. It's still at lunch or whatever was going on before the meeting.

This quick minute of quiet can be incredibly valuable, and it can greatly increase meeting productivity.

3. Don't let efficiency get in the way of connection.

It's easy for us to jump right into the content when we start a virtual meeting. If we're in person, that *might* still happen. But oftentimes we'd have some side chat in the hallway on the way to the meeting. Virtually, you don't have that kind of organic connection.

When meeting remotely, it's not only valuable but necessary to carve out time for your team to connect at the beginning of most meetings. If you're an intact team that's worked together for 15 years, that connection before content might look a little bit different. It might be more task-focused than it would be for a new group that's just meeting for the very first time.

Refer to the first chapter in this book for a deep dive on connection before content, as it's the third essential ingredient we recommend for high-engagement gatherings.

Changing Your Group's State of Mind

State of mind matters more than script or your agenda for a meeting. This is true for in-person meetings, too, but virtually it matters way more. It's one of the reasons why I take 60 seconds of silence, and why I emphasize connection before content. Both create a shared experience for everyone and a chance to shift your state.

> State of mind matters more than script
> or your agenda for a meeting.

In any group larger than six people, I like to start with at least one breakout. It generally shifts the focus from "me" to "we." And just about every virtual meeting starts out with a bunch of people thinking about themselves. Your team members may be thinking about how much *they* have to get done, what's happening around *them* or how stressed *they* are. A quick conversation with others pulls people out of the "me me me" wormhole a bit.

No matter what my agenda is, when people change their state, they completely shift the outcome of the meeting.

Yes, Body Language Still Matters in Virtual Meetings

When we meet virtually, we miss many nonverbal cues and body language we rely on in person. Still, if you're presenting or running a virtual meeting, you should be aware of your own body language. Try to be a little more physically dynamic in the way you express yourself. Get your hands up into the virtual window. Also, invite the group to shift their body language.

Recently, in a workshop with the University of California, I experimented with something new. I told the group that one of the best leadership tips I've ever received was to try to share my own failures and other people's successes. I asked others to think about that idea, and visually express how that approach made them feel. It could be an uncomfortable facial expression communicating, "I don't know if I could do that." Or they might smile while giving it the thumbs up.

I simply invited people to change their nonverbals and it had an amazing effect. In gallery view, we could see the dramatic shift from the standard Zoom face—that vacant look we all seem to have when we passively meet online—to something animated. Everyone was expressing their emotion. So much was communicated without saying a word.

It's a nuanced idea, but a pretty cool way to help people really teleport through the screen.

Share Highlights, Lowlights and Insights

When you're sharing with the group, there's magic in covering highlights, lowlights and insights. It's cool if you just share one. There's so much value in talking about what is working well, for example.

But if somebody's really struggling at that moment, it's tough to just put on a smile and share a highlight. Opening it up for the group to share not only highlights, but lowlights and insights can have a big impact. It acknowledges the full spectrum of life, so people feel more comfortable sharing what they're experiencing.

End the Party While It's Still Fun

Keep things moving. Don't wait until there's a lull. When everybody comes back from breakouts, I love to encourage people to quickly share—or "popcorn out"—what they learn.

Oftentimes that sparks a ton of fast-paced engagement. Five to ten people might share highlights and snippets in two to three minutes. But I don't want to go until it's crickets and people are just waiting awkwardly for the next person to share. With microwave popcorn, once it begins popping it goes fast. If you wait until there are long pauses between pops, your popcorn will burn. That's why facilitator 101 is to always end the party while it's still fun. Don't let the popcorn burn.

End the Meeting Intentionally

Just as you don't want to let a party go on too long, you want to plan ahead for the end of a meeting. Often, we just cut things off when we run out of time.

But we need to meet with purpose and intention from the beginning of the meeting through the end.

Group Anthem Closing Exercise

One of my all-time favorite closing exercises comes from a wonderful facilitator in New Hampshire named Nate Folan. The exercise is called Group Anthem. The idea is to have group members check out at the end of a meeting using a statement that begins with one of three phrases: "I am, I believe or I will." This encourages people to share something meaningful.

No matter your group size, you can invite people to popcorn their responses to this prompt. It's a really uplifting way to end a meeting.

Other Intentional Ways to Close a Meeting

Whether you do this or something else, you want to close the meeting in a purposeful way. What you don't want to do is frantically try to schedule the next meeting at the last minute. Don't try to squeeze in *just* a little more even when people are already late for their next meeting.

I often set a timer on my Google Home to go off five to ten minutes before the end of a meeting or session. This is to remind me and the rest of the group that it's time to pause and end the meeting intentionally.

This could be as simple as coming up with the next action steps and sharing those in chat to make sure that's clear. You could also have participants jot down action steps on sticky notes and hold those up to the camera.

3 Really Practical Zoom Tips

1. Use chat as a way to engage introverts.

Introverts may not want to unmute. But they may be perfectly happy typing something really brilliant in the chat. Inviting people to tune in that way can be a game-changer for the entire group, not just introverts.

2. Direct the energy of multitasking toward connection.

I often invite people on Zoom to talk while I'm talking. If we met in person, people probably wouldn't do this. It might seem impolite. They would probably just let me talk, and they wouldn't have any side conversations. In Zoom or any other platform, however, people can talk while I'm talking without it being too disruptive.

I give meeting participants instructions on how to multitask. For example, I might say I'm going to share three minutes of content, and invite people to share live what I'm saying in the chat. If anybody missed what I said, they can catch it in the chat. It's multitasking, but it's helping people to connect with each other and ideas.

3. **Use visual cues and breaks to hold participants' attention.** In videos, there are lots of attention resets. The same goes for the best books and movies. But when we hop on a virtual meeting, it's just one long, continuous thread that might last an hour or two.

Understanding this, I try to engage people by changing things up about every seven to 15 minutes. That might involve inviting people to contribute or shut off their video and go stretch. I might also show the group something visual and ask them to read or digest it and share their thoughts through chat.

To run a successful virtual meeting, you want to invite contribution rather than just consumption. When we meet, we want to engage and connect. We want to pay attention to our state of mind, not just the agenda. We want to remember our purpose and intention, from the unofficial start to when we end our virtual time together.

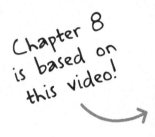

Chapter 8 is based on this video!

 Steve 1 month ago

Of all of the videos I have ever seen on YouTube to try to learn about online meetings, this video has been a combination of the most helpful and the most engaging, and the most fun to watch.

   REPLY

 Bruce 2 weeks ago

I just had to share this with someone who attends some meetings where a few have their preset agenda in mind. I think if they work on connection first they might be more likely to focus on the organization rather than their personal desires.

   REPLY

8

Do's and Don'ts of Virtual Meetings

7 Pitfalls and Best Practices for Gathering Remotely

You know and have likely experienced the unique challenges associated with not being able to meet in person. But there are incredible opportunities as well.

I'm fortunate to get to work with some of the smartest leaders and educators on the planet to help them make virtual engagement easy. My experience has helped me better understand what works—and what doesn't. My personal blunders and watching my clients' successes have informed this chapter and list.

For your next virtual meeting, here are seven tips you should keep in mind.

1. **Design Your Meeting for Contribution, Not Consumption**

   So often our virtual meetings take a nosedive before they even begin because we design them for people to just sit there and passively take in information. That's really hard to do for an extended period of time while you're staring at a screen with this pixelated, laggy talking head.

Imagine each person started a stopwatch when they spoke or contributed in some way. What would each person's total be? If the average is less than two minutes, it's possible your gathering is designed for consumption.

One of the easiest ways to design your meeting for contribution not consumption is to start off with a question. Create an opportunity for people to connect to the purpose of the meeting and to each other at the beginning of the meeting, or at least within the first five to 10 minutes.

> **One of the easiest ways to design your meeting for contribution not consumption is to start off with a question.**

Short on time? Utilize the chat, but consider inviting a few people to come off mute to expand on their comment.

2. **Set Expectations, But Don't Force People to Do Something**
Sending out a message that says it's mandatory for employees to have their video on during the meeting isn't helpful. What I do think is helpful is sending out a video, email or other written communications beforehand that set expectations for what the meeting is going to be like. If it's a recurring meeting, you can do this once to set those cultural expectations.

Personally, I like to record and send out a video beforehand that says, "Hey, everybody, come ready to have your video and microphone on. This is going to be interactive. It's not just going to be me just talking at you. And there's going to be multiple times where we'll take video breaks when we're listening. So if you want to bring an apple to eat then, feel free to do that. If you come prepared to unmute and share your video, you'll have a much more fun, engaged experience that you'll actually get more out of."

Frame the expectation from the perspective of how others will benefit rather than, "Hey, can you turn the video on *for me*, so that you're engaged?" Instead, tell your team members what's in it for them. What benefit or value do they receive from coming ready to engage?

3. Meet for Purpose, Not for Time

The approach Priya Parker suggests in her book, *The Art of Gathering*, runs counter to the way we usually design our meetings.

More often than not, we schedule meetings to begin and end at a certain time rather than planning out what we want to accomplish. Instead of doing that, I would invite you to get crystal clear about your intention for that meeting ahead of time, and meet for that purpose rather than just for a set amount of time.

If you're outcome-focused, let everyone know exactly what you want to happen when you meet. And if you finish the meeting 20 minutes early, you've just given yourself the gift of time. In a culture where we all have way too much to do and too little time, you may have just created 20 minutes for a whole group of people to go get something else done. In a 12-person meeting, that adds up to four hours of human attention, and possibly hundreds of dollars of a company's budget.

Meet for purpose and not for time. In order to do that, you have to actually take a minute and get clear on *why* you're meeting. Do this in advance, as opposed to halfway through the meeting having everybody wondering why this meeting wasn't just an email.

> ## Meet for purpose and not for time.

4. **Start Unofficially, and Don't Reward People for Being Late**

This one comes from experiential trainer and consultant Mark Collard, who knows a thing or two about making workshops fun.

Typically we set a meeting start time—say, 11 a.m.—and we wait and hang out until everyone shows up. An unofficial start on the other hand begins a few minutes ahead of schedule and continues a few minutes after the meeting's official start time. It's designed to immediately and purposefully engage people, and there are lots of ways to do this.

For example, I like to hold up a question to the camera for my unofficial start to a virtual meeting like, "What would you do differently if nobody would judge you?" I invite people to respond to that question in the chat or just by unmuting and sharing. Ideally, this exercise sparks purposeful engagement. If you want to try this for your next virtual meeting, choose a question that relates to the purpose of the meeting.

An unofficial start offers understanding for people being late. With virtual meetings, you've got the commute from the kitchen to the living room through the pile of kids, the Wi-Fi is lagging and you need to restart your computer to update to version 13.2.758—whatever that is. Some built-in flexibility makes accommodations for those challenges.

The unofficial start also recognizes that time is precious. It's a nonrenewable resource. So if you've got people together on the call, you can start immediately and create the kind of organic connection that happens in person, but usually doesn't occur virtually.

Sometimes we sacrifice efficiency for connection. But with an unofficial start, we can be efficient with our time and connect right at the outset of the meeting.

5. Do Use Breakouts—But Don't Split Into Groups "Just Because"

Just having a button on Zoom and other platforms that allows you to split into smaller groups virtually isn't reason enough to do breakouts. These only really work when you do them with intention.

Having people split up and talk with each other is a great way to make use of your time together. If you split into three breakouts, you're basically having three meetings at once. Brains are working more collaboratively.

After the breakout, I recommend bringing everyone back together afterward to debrief. That will allow you to turn those cliques into a single community. That could be as easy as having everybody answer the question, "What is something really valuable that you heard in those conversations that you'd love to share with the group?" A simple query like this may be all that's needed to harvest information from these intimate, disparate conversations. It's a great way to share what everyone's learned very quickly, and to invite and design for contribution, rather than consumption.

Do use breakouts. But don't do them just because you can. Make sure the intention of the breakout is crystal clear.

Sidebar: Check in With Your Group

Before we go on to my next tip, I want to take time to practice something that I always invite folks to do during meetings: check in with your group. If you're well into your meeting, ask the group how it's going for them.

Ask everyone, "On a scale of 'This meeting is going really well—it's exactly what I hoped it would be'—to, 'Oh my gosh, this is terrible, we should all leave right now,' where are you at?" Use the "thumb-o-meter": thumbs up, down or sideways. If you don't have video, ask the group to rate the meeting on a scale of 1 to 10, where 10 is the best meeting ever and 1 is the worst.

As the leader or facilitator, if you get a bunch of 4s, 5s or 6s, pause. Don't just push ahead and waste everyone's time, including your own. Check in with your group. Ask in the chat or verbally what can be done to raise that rating so the meeting can be really valuable. Then make adjustments and course-correct so you can have the conversations that the group needs.

6. Do Use Analog Visuals to Connect. Don't Screen-Share the Whole Time

Use analog visuals, like I do in my YouTube videos and virtual meetings. They're not only cool, they also help people connect with you. But please don't screen-share the whole time.

When you screen-share on any virtual platform, it maximizes content and minimizes connection and engagement. So even if you do have a deck to share, screen-share for a bit, but design breaks where you're going to stop sharing your screen, and invite some contribution. For example, while taking a break from screen-sharing, hold up a quote to the group, and invite their reactions and response.

Our brain is designed to encode visuals and experiential data into long-term memory. An analog visual adds a dynamic element, and actually makes us more human, as opposed to only having this little box of pixels to look at in Zoom. When we bring things into the frame from outside the box and share them with the group, it's like we're introducing people to parts of ourselves and our humanity.

In this way, visuals are a really useful tool not only educationally, but from an engagement and connection standpoint as well.

7. Close Intentionally, But Don't Rush the End

So often we meet for time, and a few minutes before the top of the hour, we realize we're not going to finish everything we set out to do. Then we hastily check our calendars to find another time to meet.

To avoid this, decide before the meeting what experience you want to do last, prior to closing the meeting. I invite leaders to end with the group's words and contribution, rather than their own words and inspirational message.

Ask everyone in the group to think about one word that describes what they're thinking about at the end of the meeting. Unmute the call, and let everybody share this. Or in the chat, have everyone type in all caps one thing they've taken away from the meeting that they absolutely don't want to forget.

You don't have to spend a long time wrapping up. But you should plan an interactive exercise for the end of your virtual meeting, so you can finish it on a high note.

Chapter 9 is based on this video!

 Lisa 3 days ago

Massively useful? YES!! This video is going to get a listen weekly until I've got it all down perfectly.

   REPLY

 Chad Littlefield 3 days ago

Ha! Thanks, Lisa. You rock!

  REPLY

9

How to Make Online Meetings More Engaging

5 Essential Ingredients to Increase Virtual Connection

OK, so let's be honest: Done wrong, virtual meetings can be exhausting and boring. Your team may already be ready to check out before you've even gotten started. But that doesn't mean you have to resign yourself to dull, passive online gatherings.

In fact, I've taught tens of thousands of leaders and educators about five ingredients that will increase engagement. If you follow these suggestions, you'll see a marked increase in participation and contribution from your group when you meet virtually.

Note: *These are the same five ingredients that I shared in the first chapter. We chose to include these here because this book is not intended to be read sequentially. Beyond that, if you master this structure, it'll drastically increase the quality of your gatherings.*

In order from the beginning of the meeting to the end, the key ingredients are:

1. The unofficial start
2. The context hook

3. Putting connection before content
4. Content designed for contribution
5. A compelling closing

1. Unofficial Start

Typically, we reward people for being late to meetings by waiting around for a few minutes until Wi-Fi catches up or the last straggler arrives. As a result, those who are on time have nothing to do at the beginning of the meeting. But there's a better way!

So what's the antidote?

Before everyone has arrived, engage participants with an activity or prompt as a casual—yet deliberate—beginning to the meeting. The unofficial start is a brilliant concept that was developed by Mark Collard, the Australian-based founder and director of *playmeo*, the world's largest database of experiential collaborative learning exercises. And it's a great way to spark immediate and purposeful engagement with your group.

There are lots of ways to initiate an unofficial start. One of my favorites is to simply pose a question. You can invite people to respond verbally. Yes, the unmute button does exist. And nobody will get hurt if they use it.

If you have a large gathering, ask participants to share their responses in the written chat. This basic exercise will allow people to immediately and purposefully engage, and warm up a little. Remember, the best way to avoid awkward silence is to create productive silence. Give people five to 10 seconds to think of their response before asking them to share.

This unofficial start should commence a few minutes before a meeting officially starts (say, at 8:57 a.m. for a 9 a.m. meeting).

The unofficial start is a way to honor the people who show up early as well as those who arrive on time. It also extends understanding for people who show up late because of computer or internet issues. When we "commute" to our home office, we may have to deal with three kids, a barking dog, Wi-Fi issues and a computer restart.

Lateness sometimes happens unexpectedly. Creating an unofficial start can completely shift the tone for the rest of your gathering. And it only needs to consume a tiny fraction of the total meeting time.

2. Context Hook

You may know why *you* are in a meeting. Yet, as a leader or educator, you can't assume everyone else does. You probably have even hosted or attended a meeting where you weren't clear on the aim. The context hook is an idea that brings everyone into the same world for the brief moment of your meeting.

In her book *The Art Of Gathering: How We Meet and Why It Matters,* Priya Parker suggests meeting for purpose rather than for time. Yet how often do we set meetings for 30 or 60 minutes only to fill that time with directionless chatter? We're unlikely to meet our goals doing this. Merely having a meeting on our calendars is hardly reason enough to engage. Participants need to understand the purpose of the meeting.

You provide the context hook when you clearly state your intention for the meeting. Ideally, you should do this in a way that focuses on the needs of everyone who's attending the meeting. Intention is very different from an objective, and it goes well beyond what you want to get done. An intention incorporates the needs of everyone.

Here's an example from a remote workshop I led with 125 executives. They were a bit resistant to the idea of having an online-only leadership meeting. So I kicked things off by saying, "My intention in the next 90 minutes is to be a painkiller for the next 100 hours of virtual meetings you'll be in." Do you see how that empathetically acknowledges everyone's pain and piques their curiosity? I knew that if I wanted them to tune in, I needed to provide that context hook.

The Latin root of the word *intent* or *intention* means *stretching* or *to stretch*. Think about intention like a rubber band that stretches around the needs of the whole and pulls people together.

Now, reflecting on everything we've discussed so far, feel free to pause for no longer than one minute. Then pick a meeting on your calendar this week, and write your intention for the meeting in the box below:

3. Putting Connection Before Content

We spend most of our time online consuming content, and very little time interacting with others. That's why putting connection first matters so much to support virtual engagement.

In the most basic sense, this is about connecting before you dive into a meeting's agenda. If you want to share content with no interaction, my advice is to record a video. People can watch it and then move onto the next item on their to-do list. But if you're meeting with people, you need to engage. Humans are wired to connect. Even the most resistant participants who prefer to turn their video off will benefit mentally and emotionally from putting connection before content.

When I talk about connection before content during a meeting, training or virtual workshop, people often push back. A common response is that there's not enough time to connect before diving into a meeting's full agenda. But I (and a large number of social scientists) would argue connecting increases productivity. It shifts the mindset of participants, so that they focus on contributing, not just consuming information. As I unpack in several other chapters, if you want engagement, you must design for it.

I like to share the wisdom of Bill Nye (yes, The Science Guy) to illustrate the importance of a connection-first approach. He once said, "Everyone you will ever meet knows something you don't." Personally, I find when I hold up that quote to the camera and read it out loud, even some of the curmudgeonly critics in the crowd come around. Everyone has something to contribute. Sidebar: This is one of the quotes in our deck of *We! Engage Cards* if you want to add those to your toolbox.

By contrast, if at your next meeting only two people talk and seven people don't say a word, you've flushed several new ideas, connections and insights down the toilet. The opportunity cost of not carving out time for purposeful connection before content is quite high.

I first learned about the concept of connection before content from author Peter Block, who's done extensive work in consulting and civic engagement. He talked about how no work can be done without this personal connection. I have since adopted, dissected and built on the concept in a variety of ways.

But one thing to be clear about is that connection before content is *not* an icebreaker. For starters, it has to relate to the purpose of the meeting.

I was recently on a video conference call where a well-meaning facilitator started out with two or three goofy icebreaker games. While the activities made a few people smile, the chat was filled with complaints about the lack of relevance. When connection is done well, nobody should have to question the relevance, since the purpose is embedded directly into the question, prompt or activity.

My go-to form of connection before content is to pose a question that's intended to be answered in groups of three to four people. I work to make sure my question allows everyone to connect with each other while also relating to the purpose of the meeting. If you're reviewing the last quarter, you might ask team members, "What was an 'aha moment' you had this past quarter? What led to that revelation or realization, and why was it important?"

After five or 10 minutes, bring the full group back together and have everyone quickly share their responses. This process increases contribution but doesn't suck up too much of the group's time.

Remember to carve out a few moments to connect at the beginning of your meeting. Energy and morale are likely to take a hit if you don't put connection before content. As I'll unpack next, your content is still typically the meat and potatoes of your gathering. It's likely going to fill at least 80% of your time together. But it shouldn't take up 100% of the meeting.

> My go-to form of connection before content is to pose a question that's intended to be answered in groups of three to four people.

4. Content Designed for Contribution

If you want your online meetings to be more engaging, you have to design content for contribution, not just consumption. That means making it more visual and experiential.

Naturally, you'll invest more time in creating content for your meet-ing than on any other element. This is your agenda. It's what you'll cover, discuss and ultimately do in the lead up to the meeting and after you disperse. But that doesn't mean you'll be doing all the work or talking.

It's easy to get into the bad habit of talking through a whole meeting while everyone else just listens. When you're meeting online, there's a great way to get out of this rut. You can do something virtually that you can't do in person: Everybody can talk and listen at the same time via the chat. This is an amazing way to harvest lots of perspectives all at once and avoid groupthink. It can also be a great way of connecting people to your content.

When you're getting into content, utilize the chat. Invite people's perspectives. After your prompt, give everyone enough time to think quietly and write thoughtfully. Then allow time for people to read others' perspectives. Nothing is more frustrating or fruitless than inviting comments from the group only to have an endless chat thread go unread. This can be avoided simply by saying, "Once you've shared your perspective, see if you can gain something valuable from somebody else in the group by scrolling up and reading through the chat for a couple minutes."

As you continue with the meeting, turn each agenda item over to the group. Frequently, invite others to react, respond or participate. This could be done in the chat, or by asking participants to unmute their microphones and share their perspectives verbally. Even a simple, "How are we doing on a scale of 1 to 10?" can break up the monotony of consumption.

Designing content for contribution rather than consumption will make a big difference in the flow and energy level of your meeting. It also makes your job easier! As leaders and educators, you have enough on your plate. You're not solely responsible for what you discuss or how meetings go. Crowdsource content by frequently inviting feedback and participation. This will improve the quality of your meetings without putting all the responsibility on your shoulders.

At the same time, there are some simple ways you can make content delivery more engaging. One pro tip: Use analog visuals to make your content come alive and encourage engagement. I might, for instance, be curious how the group is thinking and feeling. When I ask about this, I like to hold up a stress ball brain and heart I have lying on my desk. It's a lighthearted way to make the question more tangible.

Use stuff you've got lying around your home or your office for visuals, rather than constantly screen-sharing PowerPoint. When we screen-share, we maximize content and minimize connection and engagement. Any time that you're able to stop screen-sharing and get your point across with a visual you hold up to the camera, your group will appreciate it. Better yet, invite the group to go grab a prop or visual that represents something you're discussing.

We're more likely to retain information over the long term when it's accompanied by visuals. The brain loves novelty too. PowerPoint was originally created in 1987. So, although it's been updated, it has lost a bit of its luster.

5. A Compelling Closing

The final ingredient you need to make your online meeting more engaging is a compelling closing.

I once met a woman who introduced herself to me as a "professional storyteller." She was half my height and double my age with all white hair. I asked her, "What's your number one tip for telling really phenomenal stories?" Her response was simple: "Just know the first sentence you're going to say and the last sentence you're going to say. You can fill in the rest in between."

Adapting her advice, you should know how you're going to open your meeting. Plan for an unofficial start, know your context hook and put connection before content. Then, prepare in advance for how you're going to close the meeting.

Too often, we get to the end of our meeting and we forget to close with anything deliberate. Remote meetings often end with people frantically checking email and scrambling to get onto the next task. Instead of this chaotic and stressful fade-out, close with a deliberate exercise or checkout process.

Wrap up your time together with your group's words rather than your own. It could be everybody sharing a closing statement or one word in all caps in the chat describing how they feel.

For more on this, check out the chapter titled "How to Keep A Remote Team Engaged" for five of my favorite closing activities.

REMOTE TEAMS

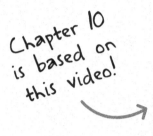
Chapter 10 is based on this video!

Courtney 7 hours ago

Hey Chad! I'm loving your content!! I am an educator where I taught elementary and junior high students for 17 years and now I'm coaching teachers. I have six teams I work with and creating connections amongst team members is a huge priority of mine. Connection creates collective team efficacy which directly generates greater student learning.

   REPLY

Birgit 1 day ago

Great video once again, Chad—am I able to use a snippet of this video with a session I am facilitating tomorrow regarding the power of asking powerful questions. Love when you share that it's about being interested not being interesting.

   REPLY

10

How to Build Trust in a Virtual Team

A Story, a Strategy and an Exercise

A massive global study on trust published in the Harvard Business Review found that only 49% of full-time employees had "a great deal of trust" in the people who work above and alongside them. This is a big deal given how trust can affect every aspect of an organization.

"Trust is like blood pressure," according to author and consultant Frank Sonnenburg. "It's silent, vital to good health, and if abused it can be deadly." I would argue that on virtual teams, we're at high risk for hypertension. But there are ways to build trust within remote teams.

I know this firsthand from working with some of the most innovative organizations on the planet and helping them amplify connection, belonging and trust. I created the *We! Connection Toolkit* for this purpose, and in this chapter, I'm going to share some of my favorite tips and ideas to build trust.

First, it's important to understand that connection is a fundamental component of trust. Other components include reliability, accountability, generosity and creating boundaries.

I agree with researcher and author Brené Brown who says connection is "the energy that exists between people when they feel seen, heard and valued; when they can give and receive without judgment; and when they derive sustenance and strength from the relationship." This definition for connection serves as the foundation for building trust in a team—in person or virtually.

> It's important to understand that connection is a fundamental component of trust.

In this context, there are five essential ingredients to building trust. Culturally, you must ensure people feel that you:

- Are willing to know them.
- See them.
- Hear them.
- Understand them.
- Are with them.

It's not just that you as the leader see, hear, understand, and are with them and willing to know them. Rather, these become cultural norms and values for the organization.

Trust Improves Performance

Several years ago, Google launched a massive research project to determine what characteristics are most important in high-performing teams. The No. 1 characteristic was the degree of psychological safety a team experienced. One way Google defines psychological safety is fostering a culture of inclusivity. You're not stifling anybody's ideas. You're inviting people to be themselves.

If you want people to really be themselves, you've got to be willing to know them. You've got to see them. You have to hear them (and they have to feel heard). You have to get them, and they have to feel understood. You've got to be with them. That means supporting and building them up.

We live in a culture where there's always too much to do and too little time to do it. What I'm going to share with you is a quick way to create a culture of trust in a virtual team.

But before we talk about tools for building trust, I want to share a story. This one is about a time I tried to build a relationship of trust, and failed—at least at first.

The Airport Rental Car

I was on a flight that had to turn back because of bad weather, and so we landed at our original airport. There, everyone who had been on the flight had two choices: sleep in the airport or rent a car and drive several hours to our destination.

There was chatter on the plane about renting a car or getting a three-hour Uber. People were talking about all different options. I thought, it's 2 a.m. If I try to drive myself, I'm going to crash. So is it possible there are a few people who can trust each other enough to rent a car together and drive?

Since I help organizations amplify connection, belonging and trust for a living, I figured I wouldn't have any trouble building some trust with the people around me. I talked with a woman who I'd sat by on the plane. When the idea came up to rent a car together with a couple other people, there was interest but hesitation. There was reticence to trust.

Most human beings have had experiences where their trust has been broken. Given that, I set out with the intent to build trust. I started to, in what I thought was a cool, chill way, throw out little trinkets of trustworthy sort of information. I mentioned this TEDx talk I gave once. I told the woman I could send her a link to the talk to prove that I'm not an axe murderer. I talked about my wife. I mentioned my son Otto.

Despite all my efforts to weave in details I thought would build trust, it was going nowhere. If anything, I was probably coming across as overbearing. That was until we got to the kiosk at the rental car place.

We had intended to each rent a car and go our separate ways. Then somebody from way behind me said, "Chad Littlefield, is that you?" I had no idea who the person was. It turned out that he had seen me at a speaking event. He starts talking about how great the talk was. He says he still uses some of my tools to create connection before content and empower people.

It wasn't until that very moment that the woman I had been sitting next to seemed to change her mind. The key? I'd gotten third-party validation, so now we were good to go.

The point is in order to create that level of third-party trust in a virtual team, you have to be able to connect and get to know each other. Trust can be awfully contagious in a team—especially when it starts at the top.

Ask Powerful Questions

How do you create these trust-building conversations? One great tool for doing this is to ask powerful questions. Adults tend to ask, on average, six to 12 questions a day. That's next to nothing compared to 3- to 5-year-olds who tend to ask about 300 to 400 questions per day.

One of the most trusting things we can do is to be interested in others. Yet we spend most of our time trying to be *interesting*. I was trying to be interesting and trustworthy to this person on the plane. But it wasn't working. I hit a brick wall. It wasn't until I had this third-party stamp of approval, and was more curious about her world and what was going on in her life, that I was able to build trust and rapport with her.

> Trust can be awfully contagious in a team—especially when it starts at the top.

Cards to Build Trust

Now I want to share with you one of my favorite exercises to build trust in a virtual team. The exercise uses visuals to make trust visible. Trust, like blood pressure, is this invisible thing that has a very significant impact on the health of your team.

The exercise I'm going to share with you utilizes *We! Engage Cards*. This is a deck of cards I designed that has quotes on one side and images on the other. This exercise uses the image side. (You can get a free digital, printable version at www.weand.me/free, or you can buy the full deck on Amazon or at www.weand.me.)

To start the exercise, spread the cards out image side up. Invite each person to choose one image they feel represents an aspect of trust that they want to share with the group.

Now have people in your group pair up or form a small group. Then they can share how the image they chose represents trust. You might also invite people to share a story about a time when a team member exemplified that element of trust.

You can vary this exercise in many different ways. You might invite people to choose an image that represents a tool they use to build trust. You can invite people to pick an image that represents one important ingredient of trust. Or you can have people choose an image that reminds them of a story where somebody did an amazing job building trust with them.

By making conversations about trust transparent, we take the invisible and make it visible. When trust is visible, we have the chance to build and amplify it.

Chapter 11 is based on this video!

Robinson 6 days ago

Loved the video, Chad! Specifically the part you said asking one question or going for 10 minutes to the gym! Small increments for long-term development, which reminded me of the books Atomic Habits and Tiny Habits. Just wanted to ask if you have any tips for engagement when people have their cameras off (and have to for privacy)? Maybe tips for the chat or other tools? Thanks!

    REPLY

Chad Littlefield 4 days ago

Awesome! Love both those books as well. Got to speak with James Clear who wrote Atomic Habits not so long ago. Fantastic perspectives. With video off, more structure is needed to create clear prompts and pathways to connection. I often invite people into "podcast mode" by having everyone turn off their cameras so everybody is in the same boat.

   REPLY

⇒ 11 ⇐

How to Keep Virtual Teams Connected

3 Strategies You Can Employ in Your Next Online Meeting

Will Wise and I exist on the planet to make connection and engagement easy for leaders and educators—online and offline. This is what we love to do.

There are many ways to keep your virtual teams connected. But I'm going to share three strategies specifically that I think you will really like and can start using to connect right away.

"Normal is nothing more than a cycle on a washing machine." This is one of the quotes I often share with groups near the beginning of a workshop. It's credited to Whoopi Goldberg and is printed on the back of one of our *We! Engage Cards*. To keep your virtual teams connected, it's quite likely that you'll have to do something that's outside the norm. You have to break the monotonous routine.

To change an embedded norm or your culture, you've got to point out the elephant in the room. If efficiency is taking the place of connection, you have to name that. Maybe when you meet you just click the Zoom link and dive right into the agenda. That may be preventing your team from having time to connect. The first thing you have to do is point out that dynamic.

You might even invite the group to comment and share their observations about the impact that routine has on them. They could talk about how it affects their energy levels, their productivity and the usefulness of the meeting. Then enlist their help to change the dynamic. Ask team members what they think can be done to break the old routine.

Now let's jump into the three strategies you can use to establish a new normal and keep your virtual teams connected.

Strategy 1: Connection Before Content

I share this often. However, in this particular chapter, I'm going to give you a unique and specific lens you can use to help your team connect before jumping into a meeting's agenda.

This is a year-long plan to create connections in your virtual teams. Yet it only takes a few minutes to put it in place.

You can do this by using *We! Connect Cards*. You can get this deck on Amazon or our website. But I also think information should be free. Good questions shouldn't be held in a vault. That's why we have a printable version of the questions in the deck available at www.weand.me/free

Pick one question to answer per week as a group. This can be incorporated into a weekly team meeting. If you don't have a weekly meeting on the calendar, I work with several organizations that have set a weekly standup meeting simply to check in and connect. If you utilize breakouts, this could literally be a 10-minute meeting.

Let your team members know what you're planning to do and why. Working remotely, everyone is spread out, and not just geographically. Their context, mood, energy levels and motivation are all over the place as well. As a result, we lose the organic connection we normally have when we work together in person.

To overcome this, tell your team that you're going to replace that lost organic check-in time with more intentional, purposeful connection time. You're doing this by answering one question per week as a team. That's it. It's a relatively small ask. Even the critics and the curmudgeons will usually go for a few minutes of well-framed connection before content.

This is equivalent to only having to work out 10 minutes a week to get healthy over the course of a year. In this case, however, all those conversations really do add up. You can learn a ton about each other. You'll come away knowing more about who team members are and what makes them tick. You'll learn about their likes, dislikes, preferences, opinions and styles. That will create communication shortcuts in the organization. An established culture of connection can even promote healthy conflict while preventing toxic combat.

The benefits go beyond just the team connecting too. Productivity always increases—to a certain point. A team can actually be *too* connected. It's like a bell curve. On the way up, you're connecting, and it's productive. However, if you become more connected but don't focus on the intended impact of that connection or a meeting or exercise, productivity can actually go down.

We specifically designed the 60 questions in the *We! Connect*

Cards to accelerate and build relationships of trust. Although they might not be everyday work questions, they're all appropriate for work conversations.

As a reminder, everyone has full autonomy and choice in how they answer the questions. This is an especially powerful disclaimer with a group. When you reassure team members that they have complete control of their response, it infuses choice and psychological safety into the conversation.

Strategy 2: The Unofficial End

I've talked in other chapters about the concept of the unofficial start. But the informal end is just as important, so let's define that here.

First, think of how a typical meeting goes. Let's say it's scheduled from 9 to 10 a.m. We meet right until the official end time, or 10 a.m. Then we cut things off, shift gears, pee really quickly and jump on our next virtual meeting.

The unofficial end takes a different approach. This is about being a little bit more responsible and intentional with the way that we block out our time. You're creating space for connection in the way a meeting is scheduled.

You can set the default settings on Google Calendar, Outlook or other calendars, when you create a meeting, to make it for only 50 minutes. When those 50 minutes are up, your meeting is *officially* over. The good news is that, according to Parkinson's Law, the amount of time that you give something is the amount of time that it will take.

Set aside 50 minutes to complete your official business. Then block out the rest of the hour—that additional 10 minutes—for the unofficial end. Use this time to connect informally as a team. You'll want to have the Zoom or Webex link (or whatever you're using) remain live for those final 10 minutes.

Many people may jump off the meeting at the official end. It's also likely some will stay on, have a quick conversation and reconnect. You can also finish up some last-minute work conversations during this time.

Let everyone know in advance of the meeting how you're going to use that time during the unofficial end. Maybe it's to wish a coworker a happy birthday, or to show your appreciation for your team.

Creating that unofficial end makes connection valid. Naming that time as the "unofficial end" removes the social pressure on your group to initiate connection, and allows you to build in time for it.

You can, as I said, create 50-minute meetings. When you meet for a half hour, you can schedule a 25-minute meeting, using the five minutes after that for an unofficial end. Alternatively, you can ask your team to block the half hour after a focused work meeting for an unofficial end.

Anything that goes beyond the official end time of your meeting that's designed to help people connect, communicate and engage with each other more effectively is an unofficial end. By doing this you are essentially saying, "Yes, we appreciate efficiency *and* connection, and we're going to make time for both."

Strategy 3: The Walking Meeting

There are a few ways to do the walking meeting, but the basic idea is this: Let's say you've got a team of 30 people. Everyone wants to stay connected in some way. A really beautiful way to do that is to get away from the screen.

> Anything that goes beyond the official end time of your meeting that's designed to help people connect, communicate and engage with each other more effectively is an unofficial end.

Plan for a "mobile meeting." If you're scheduling a meeting invite, title it "phone meeting" or "walk and talk." You can still invite your group to join via a video conference platform—just have them use their smartphone instead of their laptop.

As the host though, you should plan to be on a computer though so you can utilize the breakouts feature on the platform. Have people break into small groups to answer big questions.

- What was the highlight from your week?
- What is life teaching you right now?
- What are you struggling with?
- What are you hoping happens for you in the next six months?

Invite team members to plug in their headphones or just walk out the door wherever they are. Brains generally love conversations when combined with a walk or movement. You as the host or leader of the meeting have the ability to bring people back to the main session. Debrief, randomize breakouts again, and then send people back into small group conversations.

Obviously, the walking component is weather-dependent, and will also depend on the health and mobility of individuals in your group. Give team members the choice and ability to remain seated if they need to. If they want to break away from screens and sit down on a couch to have the conversation that's fine, too.

There *is* some magic in actually moving—walking and talking. If you haven't seen the TED Talk by Nilofer Merchant about walking meetings, check it out. You might just become a believer.

> Brains generally love conversations when combined with a walk or movement.

One fun add-on to the concept of a mobile meeting is inviting the group to walk toward something they want to show their partner. Then toward the end of the walk and talk, invite folks to turn on their cameras and share their surroundings.

Remember, if you want to keep your virtual teams connected over a long period of time:

1. Put connection before content by asking team members one question a week.

2. Block off five to 30 minutes for an unofficial end to your meeting to intentionally connect.

3. Shut off your cameras and take your meetings as you walk.

Chapter 12 is based on this video!

Annie 3 days ago

Hi Chad! How often do you recommend these icebreakers happen? Would it be okay to do them daily before the start of a meeting?

    REPLY

Chad Littlefield 3 days ago

Wonderful questions. It depends on the purpose and intention for doing them. Being sure that teams are doing some connection before content at least on a weekly basis protects your team from burning out, creates communication shortcuts, maintains a foundation of psychological safety, etc. This is true, though, only if the prompts you choose also connect to the purpose for your gathering. Hope that is helpful, Annie!

   REPLY

12

How to Build a Strong Culture With a Remote Team

5 Secret Ideas to Strengthen Your Team

Establishing the right work culture is critical when you're working remotely, even more so than when you're in the office. I want to show you *how* you can create a culture that supports high performance and engagement, where employees really want to show up.

After working with some of the most innovative organizations on the planet, I can share great examples of how you can build a stronger culture within a remote team.

We'll talk about five states of mind that you find on a remote team. Then I'll share five ways to engage employees with different mindsets to strengthen your culture while working remotely.

5 States of Mind

I'm talking here mainly about states of mind—not traits. Having this language and understanding different mindsets makes a huge difference in how you engage and connect with your team.

All teams have:

- Curmudgeons
- Critics
- Consumers
- Contributors
- Connectors

I've noticed the bulk of people fit into the critic, consumer or contributor mindsets. Curmudgeons tend to be somewhat rare—but loud. These are people who are living in a perpetual state of crankiness. Nothing you say or do is going to change their state of mind. They have a wildly negative impact on an organization's culture, morale and motivation.

Beyond contributors, you've got connectors. They are established and emerging leaders who are fantastic at helping people connect to each other and to the knowledge and ideas within an organization. They're phenomenal at their jobs and drive others to excel.

Knowing the different mindsets, you can use the following five methods to strengthen your team or organizational culture. This will allow you to shift out of curmudgeon, critic and consumer mindsets into the contributor and connector mentality. That's where people in top organizations really tend to live.

Know the Remote Challenges You Face

Remote teams have to overcome additional challenges to create a contributor and connector culture. People are isolated. Particularly in a hybrid workplace, those working remotely may feel more separate.

I sometimes think of supporting remote culture as similar to my experience healing a broken thumb as a kid.

I had to brace the broken bone. And my dad, who is in the medical field, told me to imagine that every day I kept my thumb straight, one little spider web of fractured bone grew and strengthened. Over time, you've got a bunch of spiderwebs, and eventually, the bone is strong enough that it heals.

The problem is every time you bend your thumb, you break those "spiderwebs." If after day three, you are impatient and you break your thumb again, you've got to start over back at day zero.

> You want to be intentional when you log off about offering other opportunities for connection.

Culture on a remote team is a little like that. If you meet on Zoom or another platform, and you press "End Meeting" at the bottom, it's kind of like bending your thumb. You break those ties. Then you start to rebuild them one connection at a time.

Lots of valuable connection and communication happens during synchronous meeting time for remote teams. But it is the mountains of asynchronous communication in between live touchpoints that maintain, support and reinforce the growth of remote culture.

You want to be intentional when you log off about offering other opportunities for connection. Develop norms around your other modes of communication, so those "spiderwebs" don't actually break.

To build a strong culture on a remote team, you have to create conversations that matter. I've found developing and rewarding a culture of asking really intentional, powerful questions is the easiest way to increase the likelihood that your synchronous time is well spent on a remote team.

5 Ways to Improve Remote Culture

One thing to keep in mind as you're trying to strengthen culture is that you can't *push* curmudgeons to be critics or consumers. You can't *make* consumers become contributors. You can only create an environment or a culture where they *opt into* that mindset and that space. When they do, your culture is fundamentally stronger and healthier. Morale is higher, and productivity improves when you're surrounded by connectors and contributors.

On the contrary, being surrounded by critics and curmudgeons drags people down, especially on a remote team. To really invite curmudgeons into the game, you have to set the intention of being willing to know them.

Let Your Team Members Know ...

1. **"I am willing to know you."**

    It's very easy for people on a remote team to not feel seen, heard or understood. That's why the first thing you want to make clear is that you're willing to know them. Set this as your intention.

    If you're a leader, people on your team should feel like you know who they are. That goes beyond knowing a team member's role or task focus. If you're not willing to know who that team member is, it's going to be very hard to elevate your workplace culture.

2. "I see you."

On a regular basis, acknowledge your team members with the idea "I see and notice you." To communicate this, you have to build rapport with your team.

One of the simplest ways to do that virtually is to be naturally curious. When we meet remotely and hop on video, we have the context of everyone's backgrounds. Be curious. Ask, "Chad, why is your map hanging upside down?" "What kind of plant is that behind you?" Or, "Can I meet your dog?"

Being curious about someone's environment is a very safe way to connect. You're letting that person know, "I see you."

3. "I hear you."

In order to hear someone, we have to ask questions. We want to encourage openness. When I was doing research for our other book, *Ask Powerful Questions*, I found that kids between the age of 3 to 5 ask 300 to 400 questions per day. By comparison, adults only ask, on average, about six to 12 questions daily.

Perhaps you want to hear from your team but feel like people are disengaged. Maybe it seems like everyone is a consumer—just "passively scrolling" through each staff meeting. My question to you is, are you asking them questions? Ask questions in an intentional way that shows you value the person. Team members should know that you want to know them, you see them and you value their contribution.

Valuing individuals makes a huge difference. There's a phenomenal study, which was conducted by the Center for Talent Innovation, now Coqual, that demonstrates this.

Published in the Harvard Business Review, it found that employees who felt like they belonged at work were 3.5 times more likely to contribute to their fullest potential.

At Airbnb headquarters, there's a graphic printed over a bunch of doors that says, "You belong here." That kind of messaging is helpful when you work in the office. On a remote team, however, you can't rely on a physical sign at your place of work. The message has to be embedded within the culture. You have to show people they belong in the way you engage them.

4.   **"I get you."**

This is really where people are saying they understand you. In order to communicate that, you have to reflectively listen. When your team says something, clarify and restate what you heard in your own words. You can even do this in chat or an email. Doing this can greatly strengthen the culture and connection within a remote team.

You're basically holding up a mirror to people's words. This has a profound impact.

5.   **"I am with you."**

As you use each of the tools above, you'll strengthen connection. By showing empathy, you can make it clear to employees that "I am with you."

When you come from a place of empathy, team members feel like you have one foot in their reality. You can actually describe the world as they see it to some extent.

Think about what makes others feel like you're with them when you jump on a virtual call. Do you know what a team member was doing for the three hours before the online meeting? Do you know what they're doing for the next three hours? Have you seen their space? Have you met their kids or their dog or their cat?

Being able to understand and describe a team member's world has a really profound impact on strengthening culture within a remote team. By developing cultures of connection and belonging, we encourage others to contribute to the conversation. When that happens, organizations succeed, and everyone benefits.

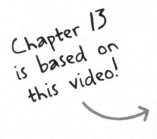

Chapter 13 is based on this video!

Jennifer 1 month ago

I'm very concerned that we are losing our connection with our peers at work, and I know our new college students are not creating those bonds and relationships that they would have if everything were in person ... so I love the idea of a podcast on a walk and then a chat afterward.

    REPLY

Debbie 6 days ago

Wow, Chad, this was really cool. I love the fact of moving out of your office. I do lots of online training (only started during the lockdown) and my biggest challenge is getting the attendees to interact with me and/or each other. I get frustrated that I am asking: So, any questions?? And you don't get the same response as when you are in live training. I will for sure apply some of the ideas you suggested in this video. Thanks for sharing it.

    REPLY

Chad Littlefield 4 days ago

Thanks, Debbie. Also, related to the silence/lack of questions, remember that the best way to avoid awkward silence is to create productive silence.

   REPLY

13

How to Have Fun at Work While Staying Productive

3 Practical Strategies for Mixing Things Up

The billionaire Richard Branson once said, "If it's not fun, it's not worth doing." In fact, he wrote a book, *The Virgin Way*, on this very premise. I don't know if I completely agree with the statement as I'm not sure that applies to all circumstances. But I do think it's natural to want to enjoy what you do for a living. At the very least, it's a noble effort to avoid drudgery at work.

In this chapter, we're going to unpack how to have fun at work while still being productive. To do that, I'm going to share three really practical strategies that you can immediately steal and adapt to use with your team.

1. Crowdsource Your Fun

What you think is fun may not be fun for everybody else. To make work more enjoyable *and* more productive, incorporate what other people think is fun.

One team member might love playing the guitar. Another might really enjoy bowling. Someone else might prefer quietly reading. Don't just guess at what would be fun for your team. Crowdsource ideas. Ask.

At your next meeting, ask everybody to jot down three things they'd like to do, putting each idea on a different sticky note. In three rounds, have team members hold up their ideas to their cameras. Take screenshots of their answers in Zoom gallery view or something similar on the platform you're using. Think about how you can weave those ideas into virtual meetings.

If somebody loves reading, you might suggest that as an alternative to a PowerPoint presentation. The team member can prepare something for people to read quietly and then discuss afterward. If somebody loves guitar, maybe they'd enjoy playing a riff for everyone as the unofficial start to a meeting.

A remote work friend and peer, Laïla von Alvensleben, took this concept to the next level. She is the Head of Culture and Collaboration at MURAL—a dynamite online collaboration and whiteboard space. When organizing a global team retreat, she actually helped to facilitate the creation of an entire remote, employee-only band to perform for the company during the big event. Like most of the ideas shared in this book, you can take them to the moon—or just borrow a quick thought to mix up a few minutes of your virtual meeting routine.

Ask team members how they might incorporate other ideas for fun as well. Could you bring the guitar into the next virtual meeting? Think about the purpose of your meeting, and how you can bring in that element of fun to help team members connect.

When you're thinking about ways to have fun at work, consider how different people approach this. Two FUNN acronyms apply here:

- **F**unctional **U**nderstanding **N**ot **N**ecessary
- **F**unctional **U**nderstanding **N**eeded and **N**ecessary

For some people, the idea of frivolous fun is not actually fun at all. They might be thinking, "I'm at work for a reason, let's get down to business." That's why you will still want to keep in mind the purpose of what you're doing. That said, if you're doing something fun that those team members love, they'll lead the charge. And they're going to be much more likely to actually enjoy the experience. When our peers are leading something, we're generally much more likely to be engaged audience members too!

As human beings, we love to share what we love. If your team has many interests, hobbies and passions, invite people to share those at their own discretion. This helps people feel seen and understood.

2. Mix and Match Your Format

Maybe you meet on Zoom every single day or every week. Perhaps you always go to the same conference room to virtually connect with your team. The structure and format of your meetings never change.

This is eventually going to get very boring for your team. Even if you think that bowling is really fun, if you bowled every morning, afternoon and night, at some point it would probably lose its appeal. Too much of the same thing becomes really monotonous. So mix up the format.

Google does this with its conference bikes. These are expensive, seven-person bikes that people sit around almost like a moving conference table. They're comparing notes during meetings while pedaling. I wouldn't necessarily recommend getting a conference bike. But mixing up the format is a great way to make meetings more interesting. Novelty sparks creativity.

A simpler way to break out of your standard format is to go on a walk. A great way to have fun and engage people is to get out of your context. Move out of your home office. Invite people to get off Zoom. Leave the conference room. Maybe grab a pair of headphones, and ask team members to do the same. Go on a walk and talk. You could even invite people to listen to a podcast. Then come back together an hour later to discuss it.

Prepare in advance for the change of scenery. If you're hoping to help your group connect, you might send people a series of three to four questions over email. Then invite people to go on a walk. Get away from the screen, and discuss their answers by phone. There is a great, free list of questions at www.weand.me/free.

Tired of the same old backgrounds? Invite people to show the team their home workspace if they're comfortable doing that.

Inviting people into your space and getting out of your context allows for unstructured connection. We learn about each other this way. An even simpler invite would be to nudge group members to join a meeting from a location they generally never use.

This kind of informal connection can spur creative ideas. People invent things over dinner and long lunches, or form collaborations and partnerships after work on the walk to the train station.

Don't wait for it to just happen, though. Create unstructured time.

There's a startup in Europe that attached chains to employees' desks. At 4 o'clock, the desks literally rise into the air, preventing people from working anymore.

Minus the chains, a company I work with tried to do something similar. Every day at 4 p.m., employees have to take a break no matter what they are doing. Team members head over to a brightly colored room where there's a Ping-Pong table, food and other ways to engage in an unstructured way.

> Inviting people into your space
> and getting out of your context allows
> for unstructured connection.

Now that doesn't work for everybody. Sometimes adding structure is really useful. But the point is, you want to make sure you're building in unstructured time for your team.

3. Script in some joy

Look at your workweek. Think about what you need to get done. Now, script in some joy. Do this regularly.

I do administrative work Monday through Thursday. But I block out Fridays to record YouTube videos. These are tutorials designed for leaders and educators to make connection and engagement easy. Through my consulting work, I get to learn from some amazing organizations, and people who are doing brilliant things. I believe information should be free, and it brings me joy to share what I learn.

Do I take *a* meeting on Friday if I need to once in a while? Sure. But my priority is to set aside that time to record YouTube videos. I script that joy into my week. Even when recording is more difficult, if I can push through to get into my creative zone, it brings me joy.

Find out what brings your team members joy, and script that into the schedule. Decide as a team how you're going to make time for these activities. Don't dictate as a leader how team members should do this. That misses the point, and it won't work.

> Look at your workweek.
> Think about what you need to get done.
> Now, script in some joy.

Lean on strategy No. 1, and crowdsource ideas for fun. Then invite people to script that fun into the daily schedule.

We're really good at keeping a schedule, right? We go to our calendars, and if a meeting is scheduled, we show up. The same goes for scripting joy—if it's on the calendar, you'll follow through.

That fun could be connected to work, or you could be taking a break from work. Your brain benefits from not working all the time. One of my favorite, goofy psychology concepts is the idea of "cognitive loafing." Really, that phrase is used in academic, peer-reviewed research. When we take a break from going, going, going, it can help fuel creative, innovative thinking. It's really useful every once in a while to just take time to have the Functional Understanding Not Necessary type of fun.

Don't be afraid to script in some joy, and leave the structure for another time.

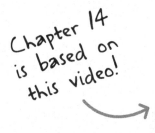

Chapter 14 is based on this video!

Bruce   4 days ago

Excellent! I cannot think of a quicker way to give people the chance to re-center themselves, assess their state of mind and set a new goal, and then to get engaged with the agenda. Of course, your terminology is much better than this. I like the fact the meeting starts differently by focusing on yourself (not the presenter). After that, I bet people will want to give something (e.g., attention) back to the presenter.

     REPLY

Niranjana   3 days ago

These strategies are simple and genius. Thank you!

     REPLY

Chad Littlefield   3 days ago

So glad to hear how helpful this was for you. Sometimes the smallest switches make the biggest changes.

    REPLY

14

How to Motivate Virtual Teams

3 Strategies to Start Smart

I have a T-shirt that says simply, "are you present?" I got it from a friend who asked me to officiate his wedding. It was a hugely thoughtful gift.

Being a professional speaker, I frequently get asked to officiate people's weddings. And, 99.99% of the time, I say no. But with this particular friend, whose name is Spud—like the potato—I said yes.

Years ago, I had told Spud a story. It was about how 15 minutes before I got married, my mentor and friend, Jeff, walked up to me. He put his hand on my shoulder, and said, "Are you present? Because you don't want to miss your own wedding." It was such a powerful question, and it transformed the experience of getting married for me.

I share this with you because it's very easy for us *not* to be present. That's true in big moments and everyday circumstances.

Working remotely presents its own set of challenges when it comes to staying connected. You and your team might be experiencing Zoom fatigue. You could be burned out from working at home or staring at a screen.

But in my work with some of the highest performing organizations and universities on the planet, I've noticed winning strategies that successful leaders implement to motivate their virtual teams. Having worked with a bunch of all-remote teams, even pre-COVID, I've learned about the nuances of coming together virtually. Operating this way differs from meeting in person.

To help you motivate your team, I'm going to share three strategies to start smart when you meet virtually. Leadership expert Matt Church talks about how our "state matters more than script." We must think about our state of mind, our state of being, and our audience's state. These three strategies will help your group shift its state.

If you just try to motivate a person—or be motivational—it can backfire. Say somebody is feeling low and depressed. The last thing they need is for another person to get in their face and tell them, "You can do it, ace!" When you try to change people, usually there's resistance and pushback.

A much more effective approach is to draw on a person's internal motivations. These three techniques help people shift its state:

1. Silence
2. Shift (the act of hitting reset)
3. Show up

1. Silence

As Cicero said, "Silence is one of the great arts of conversation." Today, in a noisy, 24/7 connected world, silence is a lost art.

You might ask yourself, what can I say or do to motivate my team? But I would turn that approach on its head. Instead of trying to motivate team members with your words, think about when you can give your group time to be silent and reflect. When your team members do that it will help them answer for themselves that all-important question my friend asked me: Are you present?

> Instead of trying to motivate team members with your words, think about when you can give your group time to be silent and reflect.

It's really hard to be motivated if you're thinking about the pile of work that's stressing you out or the fight you got in with your kid right before you hopped on your virtual meeting. If you want to motivate your virtual team, you've got to invite them to be present at the beginning of your time together.

When Will Wise, my co-founder at *We and Me*, and I have our heads screwed on right, we begin each internal meeting with 60 seconds of pure silence. We turn off our video. And we do absolutely nothing for one full minute. It consistently shocks me how much clarity of mind a single minute creates. I'd highly recommend you try this out in a meeting this week.

Go into "podcast mode" (i.e., everybody in the meeting turns their cameras off). That way they're not self-conscious or focusing on others when they're silent. Once there, mention your intention for starting off in silence and suggest they simply sit there and enjoy the quiet without feeling the need to *do* anything. That single minute can energize people—in a reflective way—and help them shift their state of mind. It'll also increase the chances that you have a great conversation with fully present participants.

As a leader, it may feel a little odd at first, and it's a bit of a social risk to initiate depending on the culture of your team. But resist the urge to pick up your phone or check your email. Be present and let your mind wander for 60 seconds. Do absolutely nothing. Sit on your hands if you have to, so you can be fully present in the moment.

If you do that, the chances that you're going to be able to motivate your team with anything you say or do after that go up significantly.

2. Shift

Now use that silence to hit reset, and help your team shift their state of mind. When everyone has turned their video off, I will often invite them to check in with their own state of mind or being or energy level.

Have team members make a physical shift that will help them change their state of mind to where they want to be. Another way that I create that shift is to say, "OK, check in with yourself." I'll ask, "What state are you currently in?" You might be exhausted, burned out or suffering from low morale. Or you might be feeling like a million bucks.

Then in Zoom change your last name to the state that you would like to be in at the end of the call. Setting this intention can have a really powerful effect. When I become Chad Curious or Chad Peaceful instead of Chad Littlefield, as I connect with people on Zoom, they're seeing that state. I'm seeing that state.

I am publicly putting out that internal intention for all to see.

That kind of social accountability is really powerful. Research has found, for example, that people run faster when they run by other people. Maybe you're jogging at a nine-minute mile pace in your neighborhood. Then, when you get downtown, you might pick up the pace until you're running a seven- or eight-minute mile. It's a really interesting phenomenon. The fact is that we all have a desire to be admired and to be liked.

When you put down the state of mind that you want to be in as your last name, there's enough social accountability to actually invite some mindset and behavior change. You're essentially saying, "This is who I'm going to aspire to be on this call."

If a leader is trying to change your mindset by saying motivational things, that's easy to shrug off. If you ask people to announce what state of mind they want to adopt, they're setting that intention, and they're internally motivated to get there.

3. Show Up

You've taken 60 seconds to be silent. You've invited your team to shift their state of mind in some way. Now, it's time to turn the video back on and really be present.

To make "cameras on" more enticing and meaningful, you might have people give a thumbs-up or a thumbs-down to indicate whether they feel fully present—or not.

A pro tip here is to show up and immediately guide people to find the option in Zoom or whatever platform you're meeting on to hide self-view. On Zoom, we spend a significant amount of our cognitive energy talking to somebody else while watching ourselves talk to somebody else. It's immensely distracting, and one of the biggest contributors, in my mind, to Zoom burnout and fatigue. The Stanford Virtual Human Interaction Lab found the dynamic to be one of the top four contributors to Zoom fatigue.

To change this, hover over your video and click the ellipses button to open the menu. Then choose "Hide Self View." Doing this will help you to be present, decrease virtual exhaustion and engage in a more natural way.

I had a teacher who always used to say, "You've got to show up to grow up." It's so true. It's hard to motivate somebody if they're not present.

More Than Starting Smart

These three strategies that I've shared deal specifically with the start to the meeting. But there are lots of ways and times to motivate your team.

Daniel Pink's book, *Drive: The Surprising Truth About What Motivates Us*, talks about three pillars of motivation: mastery, autonomy and purpose. If you want to do a deep dive into motivation, that's a really lovely read.

I trust all three of these strategies will help you start smart. The art of the start is not something to underestimate. If you start poorly, I can predict that the meeting will not go nearly as well as it could have. When a group is rooted in an unmotivated place, it takes a lot more effort to get them motivated. But if you start really deliberately and intentionally, and invite people to be fully present in the moment, half the battle is already won.

Motivation is not a one-time thing or choice. It's something we choose every morning we wake up, and each moment throughout the day. Do we put on the running shoes or turn on Netflix to binge-watch our favorite show? Do we sit back and consume this meeting or do we lean in and contribute? There's nothing wrong with taking it easy, but we have to be careful about slipping into demotivated cycles.

That's why one of the most valuable things virtual team members can offer to each other is honest check-ins. Ask how everyone is doing and mean it. No really, how are you doing *this week*? Adding "this week" to an otherwise tired question, makes it more relevant and present.

> Acknowledging what you're
> working through is empowering.

There's such a difference in asking that question with sincerity and actually wanting to listen to someone. Acknowledging what you're working through is empowering. It creates social accountability, and makes it easier for others to support you. Oftentimes that intrinsic motivation shows up when we acknowledge our own lack of motivation in the moment.

If you want more activities and resources to kick off meetings with a bang check out our *Connection Toolkit*. The Cicero quote I mentioned earlier, "Silence is one of the great arts of conversation," is included in our deck of *We! Engage Cards*, which you'll find in the toolkit. If you want to get a bunch more motivating quotes, you can purchase the deck at www.weand.me/store or you can get a free digital version of the *Connection Toolkit* at www.weand.me/free.

Chapter 15
is based on
this video!

Yuna 1 month ago

As a facilitator of many types of meetings, team building and training, this is fantastic and truly original stuff, not rehashing other ideas floating around. THANKS!

   REPLY

⇒ 15 ⇐

How to Make Virtual Team Meetings Fun

3 Tips to Liven Things Up and Take Everyone Off Autopilot

How do you make virtual meetings more fun? It's a question worth pondering because as fun decreases over time, so does morale and motivation.

As we're doing more and more remote work, it's easy to get burned out staring at a grid of pixelated boxes. Good news though. After consulting with some of the most innovative (and fun) companies and universities on the planet, I've learned some fantastically simple strategies that can make a big difference in your remote meetings.

In this chapter, I'm going to unpack three tips you can use whenever you're leading a virtual meeting. I'm also going to describe a framework for you to assess your agenda, syllabus or conference plan. If you're not checking these boxes, it'll almost guarantee that your virtual meeting isn't going to be fun.

Before we dive in, you might wonder, why should we add elements of fun into meetings? Whether for its own sake or another purpose, there is reason for us to make this a priority.

I had a teacher and mentor once who shared with me an acronym for fun. It had an extra n—FUNN: Functional Understanding Not Necessary. Put another way, a nephew of mine used to run around at family reunions saying, "Fun is fun." There are some things that just bring us joy. We don't need to unpack why. We don't need to understand the purpose behind them. They're just fun, and there's value in that.

Then there's another type of fun that is about more than our own amusement. Fun can, for example, translate into deeper engagement. As an experiential educator, I care about that type of fun too.

Fun Theory

If you haven't heard of fun theory, it's pretty phenomenal. The idea is that if you make something fun, you can actually improve performance and change people's behavior.

Fun theory is an initiative introduced to me by Volkswagen. The car company produced a video (i.e., clever ad) where a team tries to see if they can get more people to take the stairs instead of using an escalator in a subway in Stockholm.

Naturally, as human beings, we default to our comfort zone. We tend to take the path of least resistance. Most people had been taking the subway escalator. Then the Volkswagen team came in one night and turned the entire staircase into a functioning piano. Every stair you stepped on played a note. Such a fun concept, right?

The video reveals that after the stairs became musical, significantly more people put in the extra effort to make joyful (and painful) noise. Some even zigzagged, jogged, jumped up and down or danced across the keys. In fact, Volkswagen found that 66% more people than normal chose to take the stairs over using the escalator.

If we don't prioritize fun, then we risk people being asleep on autopilot in our meetings—in other words, riding up the escalator. There's immense business and educational value to making meetings more enjoyable.

5 States of Mind

To understand how to liven things up in your meetings, agendas, syllabuses, classes, retreats and virtual conferences, you've first got to know your people. Specifically, you have to understand that there are five different mindsets that people generally bring to the table.

These are states of mind, not traits. That's an important distinction. At any given time, a person can oscillate between any of these states.

These include:
- Curmudgeons
- Critics
- Consumers
- Contributors
- Connectors

The middle three mindsets above are the most common ones you'll find with meeting participants, students or staff.

Critics are very comfortable pointing out what's wrong with the meeting. They think the meeting is boring and that it should have been an email. They're perfectly content to poke holes, but totally uninterested in doing anything to improve matters.

Then you have consumers, who aren't sour on what's happening, but they're passively consuming the information you share. They're not looking to get involved. They're just kind of there, cruising.

Next, you have contributors. These are people who are not victims of boring virtual meetings. They want to add to the culture. They get involved, knowing they can increase engagement and help make the meeting more fun. Leaders can't make meetings fun without participation—it just won't work. The team must contribute for meaningful fun to be present.

After critics, consumers and contributors, you have two other types of people at your meetings who couldn't be more different. Curmudgeons are people who are just living in a perpetual state of crankiness. They tend to suck the air out of the room, and contribute very little. No matter what you say or do, curmudgeons probably won't like it.

On the opposite end of the spectrum, above contributors, you've got connectors. These are people who become hubs for contribution. They are amazing at connecting people to people, and people to ideas. They are really great at making fun contagious in any given circumstance.

Changing Minds: How to Improve the State of Your Team

The good news is that you may be able to influence your team members' states of mind—to a degree. When you look at your agenda or meeting outline, ask yourself which mindset each component might put participants in. Then put each meeting or agenda element into the appropriate bucket.

For example, if you have a meeting item that is just you talking to the team, that goes into the consumer bucket. If you're thinking team members might not like the meeting, put them into the critic bucket. If participants woke up on the wrong side of the bed, they're going to be curmudgeons. None of those categories is a recipe for a fun virtual meeting.

What *is* a recipe for a fun virtual meeting is creating opportunities for people to contribute and connect. As you set your agenda, think about what kind of feeling or energy you want to create in your online gathering. And don't be afraid to try something new.

> As you set your agenda,
> think about what kind of feeling
> or energy you want to create
> in your online gathering.

As someone who helps organizations improve connection and engagement for a living, I was curious to do a Google search on fun. I like metaphors, so I typed "fun is like ..." into the search field. The top result that came up for me? "Fun is like life insurance." Wait, what?

I couldn't help but laugh. How could this be? It didn't make much sense, and that's what made it funny. Comedy often takes us in a totally different direction than we anticipated going.

In the same way, to create fun in your meetings, you've got to do something different. You can't do the same old thing, or just make a subtle change that might not have an impact. But you don't have to overhaul your meetings, either.

Here are three simple, unconventional ways to inject more fun into your gatherings.

1. Hide Your Self-View

On most video platforms—like Zoom, Skype and Google Meet—you can hide your self-view. I don't know why the self-view is on by default. Human beings were not designed to be in meetings watching themselves being in meetings. It's weird and exhausting, and it contributes to video conference burnout.

Even worse, it puts all your focus on you. When you hide self-view, you're able to shift your focus to your team or your students. When you put the focus on others, you support a contributor mindset, and that's where the fun begins.

Research done at the Stanford Virtual Human Interaction Lab identified this self-view dynamic as one of four main factors that contribute to Zoom fatigue. The other three, in case you're curious, were:

1. Excessive amounts of close-up eye contact is highly intense.
2. Video chats dramatically reduce our usual mobility.
3. The cognitive load is much higher in video chats (i.e., overstimulation).

A teacher of mine used to say that "once you say something, half the power leaves it." Perhaps calling these dynamics will empower your group to navigate around them.

2. Use the World Around You

One of the gifts that working remotely has given us is that we have this entire life of context all around us. I can introduce you to my son Otto by simply holding up a picture or sharing a virtual background. But if we were in a conference room together, I might need to spend three minutes unlocking my phone trying to navigate to a cute, recent picture to share.

Working at home means a team of 10 actually has 10 different offices with different contexts, cultures and stories. When we share that context in creative ways, it can be deeply fun and curiosity-provoking.

In a recent workshop, I had participants screen-share a famous piece of art. Then people in the workshop had to run around their house and grab different objects to recreate that work, as a group, in gallery view (i.e., Brady Bunch view). You can't do that if you're meeting in person in a conference room or a classroom.

The world around you is a phenomenal tool for connection. I might ask you, for example, to leave your Zoom box and go grab an object that represents a part of who you are. You could also grab an object that represents something you love to do.

Our brains are actually wired to take in visual and experiential data and encode it into long-term memory. As a result, your group will be more likely to remember that moment.

3. Move

Get out of your virtual jail cell, and move. That's harsh language, but typically when we meet virtually, a couple of dynamics are happening.

One, we have the world's most phenomenal autofocus camera device in our head: our eyes. But what do we do?

When we're meeting remotely, we stare at a bright screen 20 inches away from our faces. It's letting our eyes atrophy, giving us headaches and contributing to an overall sense of fatigue.

Moving away from your screen allows your eyes to readjust. Invite people to break away. They can search around for an object that ties into the next part of the meeting, stretch or go for a walk. Take breaks to move around.

You can also create movement on the screen. One of my favorite exercises—as a warmup or coming back to a meeting—is inviting people to move and mirror what you're doing. You can do this in grid view. If you move to the left of your screen, they move to the left. If you move to the right, they move to the right. Moving and mirroring each other creates an element of fun.

Bonus Tip: Ask for Visual Cues

When you meet in person, you can hear the laughter and side conversations. You can see the nonverbal cues as well. But in most virtual platforms, everybody's on mute. It's decent etiquette but it also creates an empty vacuum of silence. You're left with only nonverbal cues. The issue is that deep engagement sometimes looks like a bunch of people blankly staring at the screen. I think about this whenever I'm doing a presentation or leading a virtual meeting because attendees are subconsciously taking in that same, boring nonverbal data from the group.

That's why I make it a point to ask people for visual cues about every five to 15 minutes. I might say, "On a scale of I'm doing really phenomenal and you're getting what you need from this meeting (thumbs-up) to this meeting should have been an email (thumbs-down), where are you at?"

Invite people to use visual cues. That could be a thumbs-up, thumbs-down or clapping. I specifically ask people to do this over video, rather than using the clapping hands emoji or hitting the like button. There's something about actually physically gesturing that creates a little bit of fun and engagement in that moment.

> Invite people to use visual cues.

Take It One Change at a Time

Erik Tyler, a friend and mentor of mine, says "Start from where you are, not from where you wish you were." We all wish that our virtual meetings were remarkably engaging and super-fun. Start small, experiment with some things, see how the group responds, and go from there.

And ask your team: What is something that amazes you? This is a really great question to pose as an unofficial start to a meeting. You can have people answer in the chat. It's a great way to kick off the meeting. You start in a place of amazement—which is a fun way to connect right away—rather than going straight into the agenda.

VIRTUAL TEAMS

Chapter 16 is based on this video!

Mark   1 month ago

Super useful as usual, Chad, thanks. I'll be threading a few of these ideas (60 Removal and Ping-Pong) into my next sessions this week. :-)

     REPLY

Mari   1 month ago

Wow, Chad, this was really cool. I love the fact of moving out of your office. I do lots of online training (only started during the lockdown) and my biggest challenge is getting the attendees to interact with me and/or each other. I get frustrated that I am asking: So, any questions?? And you don't get the same response as when you are in live training. I will for sure apply some of the ideas you suggested in this video. Thanks for sharing it.

     REPLY

Chad Littlefield   3 weeks ago

Yes, heaps! I'm actually filming a bunch at the studio today. Maybe I'll turn your question into a full video actually!

    REPLY

How to Bond with a Remote Team: 4 Group Activities

Start by Getting Curious and Asking a Lot More Questions

For the last six years, and especially throughout the pandemic, I've led many virtual connection labs inviting people to make meaningful connections even though they're pixelated.

In this chapter, I'm going to share four really simple activities. I'm pulling these activities from a sea of failed attempts to create meaningful connections. By facilitating virtual connection labs with thousands of people every month for a long time, I've learned a few things not to do and what works really well every time.

My audience is primarily leaders and educators. But I don't know your organization and your team. You know that best. As I say in every single one of my talks and workshops, I'm inviting you from this moment forward to ruthlessly steal and reinterpret everything I say, and apply it to your own context. The four activities are:

- 60 Removal
- Curiosity Ping-Pong

- QOTD, or question of the day
- Connection *to* Content

Sometimes when we think about how we can get our remote team to bond, we imagine blocking off half a day to go to a virtual escape room or something like that. That's fine and could be great—potentially. But like getting healthy, it's much better if you're able to take walks throughout the day and eat some broccoli here and there versus being healthy for one day and letting things go after that.

To create a healthy bond for your team, it's much better to integrate bite-sized activities throughout the week. That's more effective and sustainable.

> To create a healthy bond for your team, it's much better to integrate bite-sized activities throughout the week.

1. 60 Removal

The first time I did this exercise as an experiment, I was facilitating a retreat in person with a group of 10 human resources professionals. They'd all worked together for at least three years, and some had been colleagues for 10 years. They knew each other really well, and they were experiencing some cultural and personality conflict.

I took out a deck of *We! Connect Cards*, which have a total of 60 questions. I laid them all out on a table, and challenged participants to remove every single question they could answer for the group. If they felt like they could answer this question—"What are people usually surprised to find out about you?"—for the entire group, they were permitted to remove that card from the table.

You can play the same game with your group. You can have the deck shipped to you. Or download a free version on our website, www.weand.me/free, and send the link out to your remote team. The challenge, if you're playing virtual without physical cards, would be to get everybody the questions, and have them remove any they could answer for the group. But to do this, they could just type the question they wanted to pull out into the chat.

What's cool about this activity is I've never had a team remove more than five questions. I don't know if that speaks to the fact that we just don't connect and ask questions like this of each other, or it's a testament to the quality of the questions in the *We! Connect* deck. We designed the deck to feature questions that accelerate trust-building and connection, and to include questions that people haven't typically been asked before.

The questions are psychologically safe, accessible and novel. That's really useful for bonding as a remote team. A few examples are: "What are people usually surprised to find out about you?" and "If you could give one piece of advice to a large group of people, what would it be?" and "What is something you would like to do more of?"

There's a whole decade or so of educational psychology research that says when we connect to each other it creates communication shortcuts. Having knowledge of one another's personal backgrounds enhances our ability to understand each other.

For this activity, invite everyone to type questions that they could answer for the whole group into the chat. The questions that remain can be asked one at a time at staff meetings or to kickoff sessions, which leads us to the second activity.

2. QOTD, Question of the Day

Adults tend to ask so few questions per day compared to kids who are just voraciously curious about the world.

We might ask a few questions when we meet someone. But very quickly that window seems to close. We seem to think, 'I've learned enough about you.' We put that information in a virtual box, set it aside and forget it. But if you want to bond as a remote team, you've got to shift the group into this mindset of learning.

I would argue that "knowing" is usually a me-focused mindset, and "learning" is very other-centric or we-focused. When you can create that shift in a group, it's extremely helpful.

By starting your meetings with a question of the day, you can help your team connect before you dive into content. If you have very limited time, you could just have people drop their answers in the chat. If you have more time to hang out, consider splitting up into groups of three or four, discuss the question and come back together. Then "popcorn out" surprise answers and what everyone learned. That deeper version of this activity might take around 10 minutes.

You could also incorporate QOTD into an unofficial start

to a meeting. That is to say, you could ask it right before the meeting begins, and let people answer the question until a few minutes after the official meeting start time. Just hold up a sticky note with the question on it to your camera, and have people answer quickly by unmuting or typing their response into the chat.

> By starting your meetings with a question of the day, you can help your team connect before you dive into content.

You could also ask the question of the day at the end of a meeting. This gives people something to look forward to if they know every monthly staff meeting ends with a question of the day. This is one I recently used on a virtual keynote with 300 people: "What is something you would like to do more of?" I framed it as more of an application question. "What is something that you would like to steal from the last hour and bring into life beyond this moment?" That's a cool way to take QOTD and create some momentum for the rest of the day.

Think about asking it at the beginning, middle or end of a meeting. And be deliberate in asking a question for the purpose of connection and understanding each other better.

3. Curiosity Ping-Pong

I stumbled on the idea when a client came to me and said he just hated how it's the default for everybody to be on mute. It just creates this inorganic, silent vacuum in virtual meetings. How can we break out of that vacuum, and create organic connection?

Curiosity Ping-Pong is my current solution for that. Right at the very beginning of a meeting, you might ask a question like the one I mentioned earlier: "What is something you would like to do more of?" Invite people to type a quick response in the chat.

Then have people go to the chat and find something they're naturally curious about based on what that person has shared. Unmute and ask that person a question. That's where the ping-ponging begins. Let's say Kate, my wife, said one thing I would love to do more is explore museums around Pittsburgh. I could unmute on that call and say, "Kate, what is one of your favorite museums in Pittsburgh?" or "What's one of your favorite venues to visit?" And she might say Phipps Conservatory and Botanical Gardens.

In that moment, I've taken surface-level curiosity and gone one layer deeper with a question. I've also invited other people to chime in strategically. One person comes off mute to ask their question. Then whoever was asked the question unmutes and answers it.

That's the back and forth of Curiosity Ping-Pong. Let that go for as long as you would like. You could do this at the beginning or end of a meeting.

If you want to make this a whole thing, you could tell your group that you're going to play Curiosity Ping-Pong until everybody is asked a question and everybody answers a question. That would probably be practical if you had six to

12 people in a meeting. Any more than that and people might grow tired of the activity and want to play a new game.

4. Connection *to* Content

There are a lot of ways that you can connect people to your content, and make your content more visual, experiential and interactive. In this chapter unpacking how to bond with a remote team, I want to share with you one of my favorite ideas for question templates: What do you think about when you hear the word _____?

You can see how the question is open enough that you could fill in anything related to your content and it would spark a discussion about that topic.

Here's another great way to harness the collective wisdom of the group and not just rely on one person blabbing content. Let's say you're going to talk about—to pick something especially unexciting—risk management. We're going to go back to our HR group. You might ask: "What is something you know about risk management?" Depending on the group's size, you could do breakouts, answer in the chat or have people come off mute and Ping-Pong answers.

By doing this, team members can meaningfully connect to the content. In regards to creating a bond among remote employees, you're probably a team because you're working together toward a common goal. As such, while it's great to connect for connection's sake, it's really productive and smart for remote teams to connect through their content as well.

When you use question templates like the one above, you

can customize the content. You're also forced to design a session for contribution rather than consumption.

If you liked these ideas, and you're looking to help a remote team bond, reach out. Drop us a line at www.weand.me. We run virtual connection labs with people all over the planet, and we work with teams of all sizes to help make meaningful connection and engagement really easy.

Chapter 17 is based on this video!

Christine   4 hours ago

This is such an amazing idea! I cannot wait to use it at some training sessions I have coming up. I think it will really shake up people's expectations of how the training will go.

     REPLY

Chad Littlefield   1 hour ago

It's a great way to create a brain shift from "consumption" to "contribution" right at the front end of a gathering. It stacks value at the top of the hour which is too often used for "fluff."

    REPLY

⇒ 17 ⇐

Quick Virtual Team Activity: Collaborative Journaling

Use the Chat to Go Beyond Surface Conversations

This collaborative journaling idea has become one of my go-to, absolute favorite virtual team activities. I stumbled across it by mistake. Recently, I was giving a virtual keynote to 300 people at an education technology company, and I led this exercise. After the session, my client told me it was a "home run."

I got a lot of positive feedback on LinkedIn too. One person said, "This was the best session I've ever attended," and that was compared to not only other virtual meetings but in-person sessions as well.

I think the activity I'm going to unpack in this chapter was a big reason why the session I led was such a home run. Believe me, all the activities and sessions I've ever led haven't been home runs. I've made enough mistakes at this point, and I've learned what works really well after facilitating virtual team activities for tens of thousands of people.

What I love so much about this exercise is that it's super flexible. It has the potential to boost morale and make your group feel really appreciated all in the span of three minutes, or stretched out to 30 minutes, depending on how you want to facilitate it.

The other little bonus feature of this live collaborative journaling exercise is that it's super introvert-friendly. Often icebreakers or team-building stuff can get a little superfluous, and there's not a lot of time carved out for self-reflection. But that's not the case here. Collaborative journaling is also good for people who tend to be extroverted.

> Often icebreakers or team-building stuff can get a little superfluous, and there's not a lot of time carved out for self-reflection.

Learning From Failure

Now in order to share how this exercise came about, I need to tell you about a major failure of mine—or rather, partially a failure of mine, partially a failure of Zoom. I was giving a separate keynote at a university for 400 staff. I went to do 50 breakout rooms, and it didn't work. It started sending people one at a time two seconds apart.

I had this whole interactive keynote we were going to do with a series of breakouts. Now the number of breakouts we could do was reduced to zero. I had to quickly come up with an alternative that accomplished the intention and purpose of breakouts, which (for any interactive team activity, beyond this one) is to bring people together.

You want to make everyone feel connected and appreciated, and to invite the group's collective wisdom, have fun, and actually enjoy the process. In this instance, I eventually settled on the idea of live journaling. I didn't have the language for it at the time, and I've since refined it.

But the idea behind all this is that typically the chat is used for sips of connections. It's like, Hey, welcome to the webinar, where are you from? People type in their location, or some other quick, one-word, one-phrase answer to that or another question like, Can you hear me—yes or no?

Gulps, Not Sips

But Zoom has a fairly high limit for the number of characters you can type into a single chat message. And I don't know about you, but if it's a hot summer day and I'm parched, I'm not taking a small sip from my nice, ice-cold water bottle. I'm going to take a gulp. The reason you take gulps when you're thirsty is to satisfy that thirst.

> The reason we do team activities
> is to feel connected.

The reason we do team activities is to feel connected. I don't think sips and little bites of connection actually get us there.

With that in mind, I've refined this exercise to pick two songs that are instrumental, upbeat and reflective. The first one I want to make slower and pensive. With the second, I want to get things moving.

For the first song, I invite people to journal in the chat, but not hit send. For a minute or two, people are just typing based on a prompt. For the group of 300 sales leaders at the ed tech company, I asked: "What is one thing life is teaching you right now about selling virtually?" I encouraged them to take a minute and actually reflect on the question.

Think about some of the meetings you've had with potential clients. Think about some of the successful and not so successful conversations you've had. What were the defining moments? What is life teaching you? Turn that into a few sentences, or a paragraph, and when you're done, hit enter.

That was the aim for the entire first song, which lasted about three to four minutes. The next song—a little bit more upbeat, still instrumental—invited people to become miners and steal and harvest some gems from the chat.

There was so much in the chat it could have been a book. You only need to do the math. Let's just say in that two to three minutes people wrote, on average, 100 words. Multiply that by 300 people, that's 30,000 words. My and Will Wise's book *Ask Powerful Questions* is 60,000 words. That means with this collaborative live journaling, we literally wrote a decent-sized book on selling virtually in three minutes.

Writing It Down

I used the question, What is one thing life is teaching you right now? But you can pick whatever prompt will serve your group in that moment. The point is to raise the level of depth in the chat in the form of writing.

This idea kind of pulls from wisdom that Amazon has adopted, where they start off a lot of executive meetings by reading a narrative summary of whatever it is they're going to talk about. That way everybody has the exact same words and language in their brain before the meeting even begins.

Literally, it's people sitting around in silence reading what's happening. I don't know why we don't do that in meetings more often, because one of the slowest ways to transmit information is talking. You have to think about it and then you utter what you're thinking. Sometimes it's not as clear, so you double back, and people ask questions. It's just a really slow way to exchange information. Whereas writing allows us to transmit a whole lot of data in a pretty succinct format, with no "ums," "uhs" or "buts." Yet we're still using the chat for, Where are you from? Can you hear me? and other questions like that.

Now if you totally love this idea of collaborative journaling, and you need some prompts to get started, you can access 60 questions at www.weand.me in digital format for free. You can also purchase the deck of *We! Connect Cards*, and have it shipped to you.

There's something cool about having an analog visual, a card you hold up to the camera, with your question on it. But however you approach collaborative journaling, the point is to go deeper and connect to the purpose of your meeting as well as others in your group.

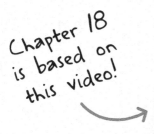

Chapter 18 is based on this video!

Kim 1 month ago

I've been struggling to build connection through virtual meetings. Thank you for your channel. I feel invigorated, inspired, and excited.

    REPLY

Chad Littlefield 1 month ago

Kim, you are a rockstar! Thanks so much for sharing. This is exactly why I built the channel. Grateful that it has been so useful for you.

   REPLY

Jorge 4 days ago

Love your content Chad. I'm willing to test "panic picture" meeting as a facilitator. :) Thanks!

    REPLY

Chad Littlefield 4 days ago

Jorge! Thanks for connecting on here and sharing. Drop me a reply to let us all know how it goes. And if you want to "co-facilitate," check this video out all about Panic Picture.

   REPLY

How to Do Virtual Team Building on a Remote Team

Low-Prep Activities You Can Use to Connect

When you think about building relationships with coworkers, you might imagine that happening in person. But many of us now work remotely, and we don't come together in an office.

So how can you do virtual team building? My intention in this chapter is not only to answer that question, but to help you simplify the approach.

Virtual Team Building Made Easy

There are lots of resources on team building. On my bookshelf at home I found a book solely about team-building exercises that use duct tape. Another book provides 52 weeks of team-building activities. Yet another covers team-building exercises specifically for STEM groups. And my friend Jim Cain wrote a book called *Rope Games* with 123 group activities that use only rope. Clearly, there are many ways to do team building. Perhaps too many.

What I'd like to do is share some activities, ideas and strategies to build and connect your team. I want to do this using only the images and objects that live where remote team members work.

In addition to all the books I mentioned, I wrote my own with a mentor Rod Lee: *Pocket Guide to Facilitating Human Connections.* We used to teach team building and leadership development facilitation at Penn State University. I now run my own company, helping some of the top organizations and universities build their teams and make connection and engagement really easy.

Leveraging Found Objects in the Remote Workspace

My favorite way to help groups work together more effectively remotely utilizes something that you actually don't have access to when you're in person. When we try to replicate an in-person style or method of team building, it's likely to fall short. Virtual is just different.

Instead, to do virtual team building, I like to use objects that exist in and around remote team members' workspaces. You can invite your group to briefly pause, and leave their computer screen—or their "virtual jail cell" as I like to call it. Have each team member grab three objects.

Now you can give prompts for any number of intentions, purposes and focuses. Here are three I'd suggest. Grab an object that represents:

- A story you'd like to share with the group.
- Somebody you care about.
- Something you aspire to or a future you'd like to create.

One of the tools I frequently use in person and virtually to help build teams are *We! Engage Cards*, a deck I created with Will Wise. You can purchase these or access a free digital version on our website, www.weand.me/free. The deck is a collection of 50 thought-provoking quotes and striking images.

If you go to the link on the back of the deck (www.weand.me/engage), you can freely access 10-plus tutorials that use imagery and quotes. You'll find some really cool group exercises there that help your team connect and promote cooperation within your team. One suggests choosing a card that represents a future you'd like to create. You can change that prompt slightly to choose an *object* that represents a future you'd like to create.

People generally surround themselves with things that have meaning for them. It's very rare that you walk into somebody's house and it feels like a hotel. People put pictures of their families on their walls. They keep little trinkets from trips they've taken. Whenever you're on Zoom, or whatever platform you're using, those "artifacts of life" are all around you. They're a part of your context. And most are hidden from the camera's sight.

> Bringing objects into play turns an otherwise boring, run-of-the-mill, two-dimensional virtual meeting into this engaging 3D experience.

Invite team members to leverage this context to interact and connect. Have them grab part of their life to share with the group. Each item is a bit like a file from their infinitely long filing cabinet of life experience. Then bring that object into the little box others see you in when you come together virtually. Hold it in front of your camera. Invite other team members to be curious about what they see.

This completely changes the conversation. Bringing objects into play turns an otherwise boring, run-of-the-mill, two-dimensional virtual meeting into this engaging 3D experience.

Through this simple yet powerful exercise, you can get quite creative with your prompts. Consider these options:

- Grab an item that has a great story attached to it.
- Find an object that represents a life lesson.
- Collect three objects that represent a highlight, lowlight and insight from the past year.
- Choose an object from the room you are in that represents your worldview.
- Grab an item that serves as a metaphor for a unique strength you bring to the group.

The best prompts are ones that will connect with your group purpose and culture.

Getting Stronger as a Team

Next, you can build on the strengths of your team and identify how you can collaborate better. Maybe you want to talk about the ways you work together. How do your personalities match and blend?

You'll need to increase the psychological safety in the group—everyone should feel comfortable opening up—and for this, relationship building is key. Other times you may want to have a bit more pointed conversation, so you need to be comfortable and open with each other.

Ask team members to choose an object that represents a unique strength they bring to the team. No prep is required. It's just a simple prompt that can have a deep impact. It also introduces an element of fun. There's a reason people like show and tell. Our brains are wired to remember visual data much better than language and numbers.

There's something powerful about sharing a little piece of your life. If you walk into somebody's house and ask about a photo on their wall, it makes them feel seen, heard and understood. Sharing an object that has meaning with the group has a similar impact.

You can prompt team members to share an object that pairs with a strength of theirs. I might show off my Toysmith Balancing Eagle that balances on the tip of my finger to talk about having the vision of an eagle. "I bring a certain level of strategic vision to the group," I might say. Or, "I'm really bad at scheduling calendar appointments and managing the details. But I can see the forest from the trees."

The brain is psychologically wired for you to remember more of what I just said than you would if the eagle wasn't present.

Using analog visuals, like objects around the home, increases retention. That's really great for team building because it makes a single moment last. You don't want to have this great moment that everyone forgets the following week. You want to create shared experiences. The more shared experiences a team has, the more cohesive they usually are.

Add "Panic Picture" to Your Team-Building Repertoire

A third exercise that utilizes images and objects is called "panic picture." I scribbled down the phrase on a sticky note when I was on a call with a client. I was working with the Virginia Cooperative

Extension. I'd sent them *We! Engage Cards*, and asked how they'd been using them. We were meeting to build on their strategies to increase engagement in their virtual training and programs. One participant shared a really brilliant idea that she called "panic picture." You can do this with images you have lying around your house, like pictures cut out of a magazine or 3D objects.

It's a great way to warm up at the beginning of a meeting. You might get to hear some unexpected stories, and have a few laughs. The directions are simple. You hold up an image or object to your camera. Then you invite someone on the call to unmute and share a story that's sparked by the image or idea.

I might, for instance, hold up an image of a fortune cookie. I'll continue holding it up until somebody unmutes and shares a story about a fortune cookie or an experience they had related to it.

This is really cool because images are like a key that unlocks memories. It's similar to when you smell something that brings to mind a past experience. Doing this is great way to get people to share stories. It leverages the brain's desire for visual and experiential information.

> You don't want to burn out your team sitting at a screen. You want them to be engaged and excited to build on what you're doing—even when you can't all be in the same space.

It's a break from the norm. Sometimes to build your team up you need to do something that you don't always do.

Using objects in your space is also something you can do quickly and easily when you have much to do and little time. In the same way, I don't suggest hours-long virtual meetings for team building. Instead, I'd highly recommend doing team building in bites and sips, rather than huge gulps.

You don't want to burn out your team sitting at a screen. You want them to be engaged and excited to build on what you're doing—even when you can't all be in the same space.

While this chapter has laid a foundation for building more shared context for your virtual team, there are dozens of creative and advanced strategies throughout the book.

Chapter 19
is based on
this video!

 Chris   10 hours ago

Chad - Love these ideas! The Green card, with the hyperlinks game ... can't wait to try that!

      REPLY

 Chad Littlefield   6 hours ago

Oooo, combo move! Love it. Very brilliant. I have been eager to test the Wikipedia game for incoming college students to have them race to get from their hometown's page on Wikipedia to the university page as quickly as possible. You could also do this for a team where you have them go from some current "state" or from a page that represents a problem to the page they want to be on. Do it in teams, and challenge the group to do it in the FEWEST amount of links possible, rather than the fastest.

 Chris   1 hour ago

This is such a fun one. I have been doing virtual scavenger hunts where I give a link to a specific spot on Google maps then ask them to follow a set of directions and then read something on a sign/ building at the new location. I love it.

⟩ 19 ⟨

How to Engage a Virtual Team

Use Colorful, Space Age Strategies to Connect Remotely

I've led hundreds of workshops on how to make virtual engagement easy, and I learn from every group and organization I work with through failure and success. Drawing from that experience, I'm excited to share two strategies you can use to increase engagement with your virtual team: one inspired by NASA astronaut training and another from a kind, creative gentleman I met virtually who lives outside Toronto.

The first method was adapted from an idea developed by Chris Hadfield. He's the astronaut who became famous for playing songs in space and making cool videos. He shares the original idea in his international bestselling book, *An Astronaut's Guide to Life on Earth*.

I'm renaming this technique and applying it to virtual team engagement. We're going to call it the 'green card' technique.

The second strategy we're going to unpack is from a lovely Canadian chap named Jan Keck. He facilitates virtual team building and connection. We're going to call the technique that's adapted from his brilliant idea 'colorful polls.'

Space Age Training: the Green Card Technique

You can't see this, but I'm currently wearing my Milky Way Galaxy T-shirt. (It features a carton of milk spilling into dark cosmic space—very tongue in cheek.) Yes, I'm a bit of a space nerd.

At NASA, an astronaut's job is about 99% training and 1% going to space. (OK, so I don't know the actual figures, but you get the idea.) Naturally, NASA is really good at training astronauts. They go over *every* foreseeable scenario. In the middle of a training simulation, green cards are used to signal random events that change the game.

> Random events change the game.

Say, for example, a bunch of astronauts are in a pool at NASA headquarters. Submerged underwater is a replica of the international space station, and they're working on a simulated exercise. They might be performing mock repairs on the space station. Suddenly, the simulation instructor holds up a green card, and announces there's a fire in the east bay. The astronauts need to put it out right away. Of course, I'm making up this particular example and not using space jargon, but that's the idea. Random events change the game.

This is an effective way to prepare people for the unexpected. I've used this in virtual meetings and with remote teams. At any point in time an employee or team leader can throw a green card. (You don't actually need to use a green card. Just find something green. Or make up your own symbol.) Again, the idea is to symbolize a random event that is about to mix things up.

You can use this in the middle of a virtual meeting. For example, if you notice everyone's energy seems to be flagging, you can hold something green right up to your camera to get everybody's attention. Then you might say, "Green card. I'm recognizing that I'm getting a little bit sleepy, so I'm assuming that is true for some of you." Then you might suggest taking a quick break to play the Wikipedia game.

If you're not familiar with the Wikipedia game, you pick two random, completely disconnected words or concepts. You might pick, say, Genghis Khan and the color blue. Then have everybody go to Genghis Khan's Wikipedia page. The goal is to get from that page to the Wikipedia page for the color blue without typing anything. Team members can only click hyperlinks to get from one place to the next.

This serves as an active attention reset. It's a random example, but it illustrates the point that doing *anything* considerably different from your current cadence, topic or energy level will reengage the group.

To recharge another way, you could hold up the green card and have everybody shut off their video. Be on mute for two minutes. Stretch, and do something physical that raises your heart rate at least 10 beats per minute. We know that the brain learns better when there's more blood flowing through it. You need to vary your cadence in meetings. The longer you meet as a team, and the more years you've worked together virtually, the more you need to mix it up.

Colorful Polls

This idea is so simple, flexible and brilliant, and can be used in lots of contexts. Thanks to Jan Keck for introducing the concept to me.

One of the most important aspects of virtual engagement is inviting contribution from your team. If your team is just passively consuming what's happening in a meeting or they go from one meeting to the next without saying anything, you can expect disengagement.

> One of the most important aspects of virtual engagement is inviting contribution from your team.

Depending on the size of your team, it's not always possible for everybody to speak or share in a really significant way. You can, however, still create small but meaningful ways for people to contribute.

Per the name, the colorful polls exercise uses any object around the person's computer station that's colorful. You get to choose the colors. It's a creative way for people to have a vote. You could say if you like chocolate ice cream, hold something blue up to your camera. If you like vanilla more than chocolate, hold up something green. You're just attaching meaning to colors.

Pick two to three colors that mean different things. You could put these on a slide and invite people to go find an object of the same color or an object that has all of those colors. Then use that to participate in a multi-color poll.

Switch into gallery view in Zoom or whatever platform you're using to meet. Go through a series of prompts to gauge the group's feedback or perspective on a topic.

Three colors that are really simple to use are—like a traffic light—red, green and yellow. Utilizing these colors is a great way to make decision-making visual and quick.

You could say, "We've talked about this idea for the last 50 minutes. Just to check the pulse, are you a green light—you want to move forward with the idea; a yellow light, maybe it'll work, but you think it needs to be tweaked; or a red light—this is a very bad idea? Can you just hold that color up to your camera?"

You can see if the screen turns red, green or yellow, or is split. This gives you a quick visual sense for how to proceed. Colorful polls produce cool visual effects as well. It's much more visually interesting than launching a poll in Zoom, or another platform or app.

Now obviously this kind of "polling" is more qualitative. You're not likely to have everyone freeze and take a screenshot to count votes. But the idea is to turn a poll into a color, and make your polls visual. It's amazing how that invites people to share their voice in a very simple yet creative way.

With even 60 seconds of preparation, these two colorful methods will add some new life and engagement to your meeting, training, workshop or virtual conference.

Chapter 20 is based on this video!

Jan   2 weeks ago

I'm going to try a version of this in a coaching session real soon and I'm stoked. Conversations with intention go much further than "meeting for the sake of meeting," so I love embedding that into topics. BIG shout out for sharing the digital toolkit for free! This has helped me engage with teams virtually in a much more memorable way.

     REPLY

Chad Littlefield   2 weeks ago

Jan, thanks so much for commenting. Love hearing how practical and useful this is for you. Without clear intentions on the table, it is quite difficult to get on the same page! Looking forward to crossing digital paths again soon.

Jan   2 weeks ago

In case it helps anyone else that finds themselves here—this worked really well as an intro activity. It was also valuable when I brought it back later in the session with the same quote/picture combos for folks to relate it to coaching. I think it bridged some gaps and gave people more insight into meaningful conversations. 10/10 would use again.

⇒ 20 ⇐

How to Engage a Virtual Team: Inspiring Intentions Activity

Break Up the Monotony and Help Your Group Connect with this Exercise

This is the first chapter and activity in a four-part series on exercises that help improve virtual team engagement. This chapter and the next three chapters correspond with YouTube videos I've created on engaging virtual teams, where I facilitate four different exercises.

I'm all about helping business leaders and educators increase connection and engagement in their teams. In this chapter, I'm not only going to share how you can do this, I'm actually going to facilitate an activity I call Inspiring Intentions.

You can simply read on and learn how to do this with your team. Or you can jump ahead to the **Getting Started** section below, and read some of the wording and framing I would use to facilitate this exercise for your group. (Just read it over ahead of time, then follow my lead.)

Having led group activities like this a lot, I have a particular way I facilitate engagement. I use certain phrases and approaches that I've found work well. Feel free to steal these, repeat what I say and use my methods in your meetings. Better yet, find some inspiration in the language and make it your own.

Green Cards: Disrupting the Same Old Disengaging Meeting

As I mentioned in the last chapter, I'm taking a page from NASA here by using "green cards," like what's done in training simulations. In this context, a green card is basically a random event that changes the same; this requires everyone to be on their toes.

You're probably not training your group for space travel, but the approach still applies, and I've adapted the exercise for our purposes. This concept of green cards is a great way to mix things up when you want to engage your team. What is really disengaging is repeating the same monotonous activity day after day.

> What is really disengaging is repeating the same monotonous activity day after day.

Click the same link.

Join the same meeting.

Show up with the same people.

Have the same small talk.

Humdrum.

Throwing a green card disrupts this monotony. That increases engagement. This particular activity—Inspiring Intentions—is really good for the beginning of a meeting or the start of a new season, project or class. It allows people to focus on their intentions.

The exercise comes from and utilizes a deck of cards we created called *We! Engage Cards*. You can get this deck for yourself and use it with your group, or you can get one for everybody on your team.

When everyone is playing with the same deck, and can hold up cards of their own, that creates a really fun, novel point of connection in a virtual or hybrid environment.

That said, you can also access a printable, digital version of the deck totally free at www.weand.me/free, and send the link to your team for this activity.

Now, we're ready to go. Below in *italics* is the actual phrasing I might use when speaking to a group to help frame and lead this exercise. In between, there are some facilitator notes that offer helpful variations or ideas as well.

Getting Started

I want to spark disruption and change the normal flow of your meeting or class. What I'd love to do is tune into what our intention is for this time. The word intention comes from the Latin root meaning to stretch. I love this because really great intentions stretch to encompass the needs of everybody in the group, and pull people together, whereas an objective is typically very focused on what you as the leader may want to achieve. Intentions have a different level of empathy that incorporates the needs of the group.

That's why we're going to start with an exercise called Inspiring Intentions. If you have the We! Engage Card deck lying around, now is a good time to grab it. If you don't have the deck, you can still access it digitally using the link above. Or find an image, object or quote on your own.

What I'm going to do now is invite you to take a minute. Choose a card with a quote or image that represents an intention you have for your time today. I've picked an image of a group of people traversing a mighty sand dune in the desert. Tying into that image, I might choose to say, "My intention today is to really lean on the support and help of my colleagues because I'm taking way too much on myself. So I'm going to be asking for your support and help throughout this meeting as we map out this future project." You see how that ties into the image.

Your intention could connect to a quote. I've chosen one from author Richard Bach, "Every problem has a gift for you in its hands." To go along with this, you might say, "My intention is to see all the challenges, roadblocks, obstacles, annoyances and frustrations as potential gifts." You might think about how you can begin to reframe and adapt these obstacles. Focus on having that positive lens, as opposed to seeing these difficulties as roadblocks that stop you in your tracks. You can shift your intention to see possibilities rather than closed doors.

Do you see the magic that can happen when you get really clear about your intention and you share it with others? Oftentimes we have intentions that affect other people. But rarely do we share them with those people.

Note: You may want to specify context for the intention, or ask participants to decide this. For example, is it an intention for the year or for their next all-staff meeting?

Take a 60-Second Break

Now, if you're leading this exercise, stop. Take a quick break. Spend 60 seconds finding a quote or an image that represents an intention you have that you'd like to kick out to the group. Done?

Beautiful. Welcome back. If you have a quote or image in hand, it's time to share it.

On Zoom or whatever platform you're using to meet with your team or group, hold that quote or image up to your camera. Use gallery view or something similar, so that you're able to see everybody else doing this as well.

Next, what we do depends a little on your group size. If you have a smaller group, I'd love to have people quickly share, or "popcorn out," their intentions. If you have a bigger crew, let's break it up.

The instructions for Inspiring Intentions are on that card in the *We! Engage* deck. Split into groups of three to five people. Have everyone share their intentions in their small groups. Then talk about aligning those intentions. Take those three to five different intentions (one shared by each group member), and come up with one overarching intention per small group. When everyone comes back from breakouts, have each group share that larger, agreed-upon intention.

Take time to discuss these intentions as a full group.

My hope is that these discussions were really useful. When we share our intentions, we start meeting for purpose, rather than time. Typically we get in this rut of filling the time from when the meeting begins until it ends, rather than paying attention to why we're meeting. By understanding your intentions and hearing others share theirs, you can connect better with what you want and the overarching group purpose.

For Your Review

If you've just been reading this chapter to learn about how to facilitate this activity, have an awesome time doing the exercise with your group. It's amazing how a small adjustment can substantially increase engagement. Getting clear about your intention and sharing it with the group is a core ingredient to increasing engagement in a virtual team.

> Getting clear about your intention and sharing it with the group is a core ingredient to increasing engagement in a virtual team.

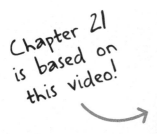

Chapter 21 is based on this video!

 Mark 5 days ago

Love it Chad—thanks for sharing. I can see this working in my keynotes: display a series of images, pause when someone raises their hand, etc., that side of the auditorium gets a point, etc. You get the idea. :-)

   REPLY

 Chad Littlefield 4 days ago

Super fun spinoff! Could work virtually too. Could divide the group by last name or birth month. Whoever gets the most points wins.

  REPLY

·≈ 21 ≈·

How to Engage a Virtual Team: Panic Picture Activity

Spark Your Team's Memory and Increase Connection with this Rapid-Fire Exercise

In this chapter, I'm going to show you how to lead a really fun activity I adapted from an idea a client gave me. The exercise is called Panic Picture. It's a great, fast-paced way to increase engagement, spark some laughter and create connection on your virtual team.

You can take what you learn, adapt that and lead the activity yourself. Or you can jump ahead to the **Getting Started** section below, and read how I might facilitate this exercise for your group. (You could also read it over ahead of time, then adapt my framing and directions to suit your context.)

For this exercise, I use a deck of *We! Engage Cards* that we created, and you can do the same. The cards have images on one side and quotes on the other. It's a super useful deck that supports tons of activities to engage your team in person and virtually. You can purchase the deck or access a free digital version at <u>www.weand.me/free</u>. You can also adapt the exercise to use objects and images around your home or office.

Now we're ready. Below in *italics* is the actual phrasing I might use when speaking to a group to help frame and lead this exercise. In between, there are some facilitator notes that offer helpful variations or ideas as well.

Getting Started

When playing Panic Picture, your only goal as a group is to score the maximum number of points. You can score up to 10. You score a point every time somebody unmutes within a five-second window to share a story sparked by the image shared.

Before we get into it, I'll give you an example of how you can score a point. I might hold up an image from the We! Engage deck of one scuba diver assisting another. Somebody needs to unmute within five seconds—since we're going to be switching images that frequently—to share a story or memory sparked by the image. I might tell you about the time I almost got my entire arm stuck under a rock reaching for a lobster while scuba diving in Massachusetts.

If somebody unmutes within that five seconds and shares a story, your group gets a point. If, however, I flip to the next picture before anybody unmutes to share a story, you can't get that point.

We'll go through 10 images. (See the list below, and have your cards ready.) You can hold up the We! Engage Cards I describe—or others—as we go along.

Note: To actually see the images listed below and watch a video of me leading this exercise virtually, go to www.weand.me/engage.

1. *coffee. Did anyone unmute within five seconds to share a story inspired by this image? Pause only for shared memories. Then hold up each subsequent image in rapid succession—every five seconds—until you run through 10.*
2. *a hot air balloon*
3. *a sheet of music on a lectern in a concert hall*
4. *Earth as seen from the moon*
5. *a van on a dirt road, driving off into the sunset*
6. *a person dwarfed by a sequoia tree*
7. *a dog (a Weimaraner)*
8. *a zebra*
9. *colored pencils*
10. *a couple holding hands*

Alright, how many points did you get? If you got 10 points, lovely. If you want to go through this exercise again at any time, you can use 10 other images.

There are 50 images in the *We! Engage Cards*—the free digital version and the actual physical deck. You can also do Panic Picture with objects.

> **Visuals cue our memory.**

Sparking Memories and Connection

The idea with Panic Picture is that visuals cue our memory. These images act like a key that opens a file cabinet of life experiences, stories and moments. You could just gather 10 objects from around your house, and hold them up to repeat this activity.

If the group didn't get 10 points this time, feel free to try the activity at another meeting to see if they can get the maximum score.

If you want an added challenge, switch the pictures every two seconds, rather than every five. And if your goal is deeper connection rather than a simple, engaging energizer, you could invite people to share more in-depth stories as well.

I hope Panic Picture gets your meeting off to a beautiful start. Maybe it will serve as an exciting interruption during your virtual conference. Or perhaps it'll become a welcome way to mix up regular all-staff meetings.

You can use activities like this one, which are geared toward engaging your virtual team, to decrease boredom and exhaustion. That'll ensure you can end your virtual meetings feeling energized and not fried.

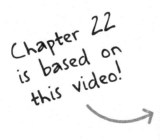

Chapter 22 is based on this video!

We!

Norma   2 weeks ago

This is going into my next board meeting! Such a great way to get to really know people!

      REPLY

Chad Littlefield   1 week ago

Thanks! Love sharing info that makes connection easy. Even happier to offer open access to it.

     REPLY

22

How to Engage a Virtual Team: Visualizing Values Activity

Use Objects or Images to Share What Matters to You and Your Team

In this chapter, I'm going to teach you about an activity called Visualizing Values.

You can read on and learn how to lead this activity with your team or class. *Or* you can jump ahead to the **Getting Started** section, where I actually write a narrative, framing and directions for the activity as if I was leading the exercise for your group. You can watch me lead this virtually at www.weand.me/engage.

This activity works great whether you have a team of four, 40 or 400 people. I would just say that as you get to larger group sizes, like for a virtual conference, you definitely want to weave in intentional breakout time.

The Visualizing Values exercise comes from the *We! Engage Cards* we created, though you don't have to have the deck to do the activity. The deck has 50 cards with images on one side and quotes on the other. The cards are a really practical resource to help you visually engage your team virtually or in person.

You can facilitate the exercise with one deck for yourself, or if everyone in your group has *We! Engage Cards*, they can all use their cards to participate. That's a cool way to connect when everyone has a deck of their own that they can use. That said, it might not be reasonable for you to get a *We! Engage* deck for everybody. So as an alternative to the cards, anytime I suggest choosing an image, you can invite your group to choose an object instead. In fact, as I narrate this exercise, I'll suggest choosing an image or an object.

Now, we're ready to go. Below in italics is the actual phrasing I might use when speaking to a group to help frame and lead this exercise. In between, there are some facilitator notes that offer helpful variations and ideas as well.

Getting Started

Alright, let's jump in! We're going to spend a quick minute visualizing values. The reason I want to do this is because "values are like fingerprints," as Elvis Presley once said. Everybody's values (and fingerprints) are unique, and we leave them all over everything that we do.

Given that, there's immense value in connecting to what we value. We prioritize what's important to us. When the word "priority" came into the English language, it was singular. Just one priority. Not priorities. But today we're living in a culture where we have way too much to do and too little time. You might feel multiple items are vying for the first spot on your list. We have so many competing priorities, it can be overwhelming.

Oftentimes we focus on everything we have to do. But we neglect to understand why we're doing what we do. We don't connect to the underlying values that shape what we create and build as a group.

What I'd love for you to do is to take a moment. Choose an image or an object that represents a value you hold. This should be something that's really important to you as a member of your team. This isn't an object that's just of value to you, like a picture of your family. Instead, we're talking about choosing an image or object you can use as a metaphor for something you value.

Visuals tend to get encoded into long-term memory. They stick. Six months from now, you'll recall some of the visuals from this exercise. Whereas a simple conversation about values is more likely to flutter away after a quick stay in our short-term memory.

Note: As the facilitator, share an example. Imagine I'm holding up an image of a fortune cookie.

In this case, I really value looking ahead and actively creating the future. On the other hand, I don't just want to be a victim of whatever is written on the inside of a fortune cookie. In regards to how this relates to the group, I might say, I think actively creating a vision is important for this team. If we just let ourselves get disrupted, rather than being the disrupters, we might not be around for long.

You can see, in that example, how I'm sharing a value I have paired with an image. Now, in a moment, I want you to go on a virtual scavenger hunt to find an object that represents a value you have. If you have the deck of We! Engage Cards lying around, feel free to just choose an image instead for this.

You've got 60 seconds. Ready, set, go!

Alright, now you have your image or object. Go ahead and hold it up to your camera to share it with your group. Look around in gallery view to see what people chose. Discuss what you brought back and how it relates to something you value as a group.

If you're a smaller team, feel free to go around the group. Not sure where to start? I believe that going in alphabetical order saves lives in virtual breakout rooms. At the very least this prevents awkward stumbling and wasted time. Try going in alphabetical order by first name, instead of fighting over who goes first, or next.

> By mixing things up in an intentional, purposeful way, you can increase engagement and connection within your virtual team.

If you're a bigger crew (larger than seven people), I'd highly recommend doing breakouts.

Remember that the way we listen often changes what people say. Don't worry about what you're going to share. Be totally tuned into what your group members are saying.

This exercise and others like it are all about disrupting your normal flow and getting out of the routine. By mixing things up in an intentional, purposeful way, you can increase engagement and connection within your virtual team.

Chapter 23 is based on this video!

We!

Jack 4 days ago

Chad, thank you for ALL THE VIDEOS this year. I work at the Philadelphia Outward Bound School, and we were really wondering at the beginning of the year if we were going to be able to continue running programs this year. You and your constant stream of great videos were a HUGE resource for us to be able to successfully adapt our program model to the virtual world. Thank you, thank you, thank you.

   REPLY

⟩ 23 ⟨

How to Engage a Virtual Team: Quick Quotes Activity

Make a Deeper Connection by Sharing Powerful Words that Resonate with You and Your Team

It's amazing how engaging quotes can be. I had a mentor who used to say "a choice of words is often a choice of worlds." A single statement or quote can shift our whole perspective. In this chapter, I'm going to share how you can use quotes to really engage your group while remote.

Also, if you jump ahead to the **Getting Started** section, I have written my framing and directions for this exercise, which is called Quick Quotes. You can read along and adapt that script to fit your group and personality.

This exercise is a proven strategy to increase engagement online and offline. While you can certainly tailor it to your group, I've tested the activity with thousands of leaders and educators. I help some of the top organizations on the planet make connection easy, so this isn't something I just pulled out of my pocket and thought might work. It's been field-tested and tailored for you. And the impact it has on engagement in a given moment is immense.

Keep in mind that none of the exercises (or any activity for that matter) is a solution for chronically low morale or engagement. But they all can provide a boost and an attention reset for sure!

Sharing Quotes to Create Connection

You only need Google to lead the exercise. However, I'm going to be utilizing and sharing a variety of quotes from a deck of cards we created called *We! Engage Cards*. As the name implies, this is a really great resource to *engage* your team.

You can order the physical deck, but you don't have to. You can download a free digital version at www.weand.me/free. If your team members don't have *We! Engage Cards*, send this link to them as well ahead of the exercise.

I'm going to be inviting people to choose quotes. Then we'll have some discussion around them in a creative, gamified way. The Quick Quotes exercise is really great for creating connection before content. Yet it can also be used as a closing or debrief exercise too.

Often when we try to *get* engagement from a group, it actually borders on manipulation. We're trying to get team members to do something that they may not feel like doing. But when you can create and foster a culture of connection, it's different. Having a clear intention for doing any activity and sharing it with the group goes a long way toward this end.

The Quick Quotes idea offers a bit of disruption in your typical flow of meetings. Meetings are usually filled with words, right? We say *a lot* in any given meeting. In fact, if somebody is talking most of the time in a 60-minute meeting, they might say roughly 9,000 words when speaking at the average rate of conversation, which is about 150 words per minute. (That's according to the National Center for Voice and Speech.) Only this is a monologue.

That's one reason we love quotes. It's a way to get to the point. A short profound statement can make you stop and reflect. Whether the quote is particularly insightful, witty or outlandish, a well-crafted sentence causes our brain to process things a bit differently.

Below in *italics* is the actual phrasing I might use when speaking to a group to help frame and lead this exercise. In between, there are some facilitator notes that offer helpful variations or ideas as well.

Getting Started

To begin Quick Quotes, if you've got We! Engage Cards, grab a handful with quotes on them. Alternatively, if you don't have the cards, you can Google quotes. Choose a quote that represents an idea you care about or believe in.

If your quote is on a card, hold it up to your camera to share. If you Googled it, type the quote in chat on Zoom or whatever platform you're using. What I'd love for you to do as a group is to fill the chat thread with quotes. When you're meeting virtually, everyone can speak at the same time by typing. By scrolling up the chat you can also "listen" to what everybody has shared.

Feel free to go completely off script once your group has shared quotes. You can have people break out and have discussions about what was shared. But what I'll invite you to do is a little quote swap.

Find a quote that somebody else shared that you believe in and connect to in some way. Then what I'd love for you to do is unmute. Read the quote that stuck out to you and tell that person what, in particular, resonates with you about the quote they chose.

One of the cool things about sharing what we really believe in is that we find other people who believe in the same things. That's much more engaging than discovering surface-level commonalities, like that you live in the same state as someone else. Learning about what others value is an amazing way to make deeper connections.

> Learning about what others value is an amazing way to make deeper connections.

There is something neat about seeing quotes in written form. But the impact really lands when they're verbalized in a group. We're taking wisdom, something shared recently or long ago, and we're bringing it back to life. This idea, too, that a choice of words is often a choice of worlds can come alive when we share and reflect the quotes that really resonate with us.

Other Activities to Increase Engagement

This is the last of four chapters on activities to engage virtual teams. I hope this was really useful to you.

I'd highly recommend also checking out the previous three chapters which highlight other exercises to increase engagement. These are great activities to improve connection with your virtual team.

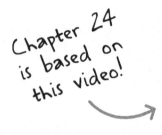

Chapter 24
is based on
this video!

Margarita   5 days ago

Hi Chad, thanks for your videos. I really enjoy them and learn a lot. I am a teen coach and now do my sessions online. I find that an extra challenge and have been looking for ideas online and I really love your contributions. Regards from Mexico...

     REPLY

Chad Littlefield   5 days ago

I so love hearing this, Margrita! Thanks for connecting in the comments. Glad to have you here. Bienvenido!

    REPLY

$\Rightarrow$ 24 $\Leftarrow$

How to Keep a Remote Team Engaged

5 Closing Exercises to Wrap Up and Stay Connected

Often meetings just end. We don't have a plan. We just break up and move onto the next thing, and it's not great for engagement. That's why in this chapter, I want to focus on closing exercises.

This is often a way to signal at the end of one meeting, what the next meeting will be like. It can serve as motivation as well as providing an idea of what's to come. If you end one meeting feeling stressed, overwhelmed, burnt out and unmotivated, you're unlikely to feel energized, alive and creative going into the next meeting.

Taking a page out of Stephen Covey's popular book, *The 7 Habits of Highly Effective People*, the best way to engage a remote team is to "begin with the end in mind."

Closing Exercises to Keep Your Team Connected

You might be wondering, where did these closing exercises come from? I didn't just randomly create them while crossing my fingers and hoping they would work.

I get to consult with and lead workshops for some of the most innovative universities and organizations on the planet, and one of my current clients is the National 4-H Council. I'm helping them design more engaging training sessions and education materials to develop young leaders.

While meeting with their leadership, we went over closing exercises for training sessions. I brainstormed ideas from previous workshops I've led, having experimented with different ways to end meetings. We picked a list of really great closing exercises, and I want to share some of those with you.

Remembering What Happened First and Last

Another reason I want to focus on closing exercises has everything to do with how we learn. We tend to remember what happens first and last in a given session or class. Psychologists call this the Primacy/Recency Effect.

Now, imagine that you're used to rushing at the end of your meetings. You conclude by just hastily scheduling the next meeting or saying "gotta go" as you look for the "end meeting" button. A much better use of the last five minutes is to engage in intentional closing exercises. There are hundreds of ways to close with purpose. The important thing is that you do *something* other than a rushed "hard stop" or worse, continuing past the allotted time for who knows how long.

> We tend to remember what happens first and last in a given session or class.

Below are five of my favorite exercises for wrapping up a meeting or gathering with purpose. Feel free to adapt this to best suit your needs and context.

1. Application Anchors

Let's say you have a meeting, and after it ends, you have nothing you can apply from the meeting or no action steps you plan to take after it's over. Well, I can tell you that meeting was a total bust.

To ensure action, a short exercise like this one can make your time together so much more productive.

Five minutes before ending the meeting, have your team break away from their computers. Ask everyone to step away from Zoom or whatever platform you're on and find an object in their home or wherever they are. This should be something that represents one application they're taking away from the meeting or an action step they want to take after the meeting.

For example, I keep a squishy, stress ball-like ear on my desk to remind me to listen better. Anyway, let's say you find an object like this. You might say, as a leader, that you're committing to being more deliberate about listening to team members before sharing your ideas.

The value in this kind of tangible exercise is that the brain is wired to encode visual data into long-term memory. A closing exercise like this is a powerful way to finish a meeting on a high note.

This way, everybody leaves the meeting with a visual cue of what they are committing to in the next week, month, quarter or semester.

2. Future Me

For this one, I'm going to take you to futureme.org. This beautiful site allows you to write a letter to your future self—digitally and for free.

It offers a really great way to close a meeting on a high note. Think about the next time your team is gathering. Let's say that's November 9. Go ahead and invite people to type a letter to be delivered on November 8—the day before the meeting. Write a letter that you would love to receive to get mentally prepared for that meeting. It could be something you want to tell yourself, or that you want to share with your team at your next meeting.

Besides meetings, this is perfect for online classes or remote learning. Schedule a letter filled with fresh takeaways and key points to be delivered the day before a test for example. If you are onboarding new team members, it's a great exercise to have them write a letter after Day One to be delivered after their first full year of work.

Having people write a letter to themselves in the future is a brilliant way to crowdsource remote team engagement. As a leader, you don't want to be the one pushing engagement. Instead, it's best to create opportunities for the team to contribute and engage on their own terms.

Team members get to choose what they write, and when the letter is sent. You type in your email address at futureme. org. You don't get added to some marketing list. You click "send to the future," and voila—your message is queued up and waiting to be sent at the time you selected.

Now that you know about this, you'll figure out a whole variety of ways to use it.

3. Question Quest

Meeting remotely, it's likely you come together a bit less often and that more time elapses between each meeting. That leaves you with the challenge of figuring out how to carry momentum from one meeting to the next. This is a really great exercise for that.

It's also a bit of a wordplay. The first part of the word *question* is, of course, *quest*. This exercise encourages people to formulate one question you'd like to consistently ask yourself until the next meeting. Then you go on a quest of sorts, seeking to answer that question.

In theory, a really good question allows you to explore possibilities. You journey, in a way, into unknown territory. You're on a quest to uncover new ideas and perspectives and you make new connections with people.

Take this question, for example: What is something you know really well? What if you were to turn this question into a quest? Ask five colleagues to consider this question between now and your next meeting. If your entire group was to do that with a question of their own choosing, connection, learning and engagement would increase significantly.

Very simply, at the end of your virtual gathering, you can have team members formulate the questions they want to ask. These could be questions they seek answers to themselves or that others pursue. It's a really lovely way to invite people into meaningful conversations.

The whole exercise only takes a couple minutes, and that's all you need to engage your team. Then you can keep them connected until the next meeting.

Building on the first three exercises, the next two are called You Can Quote Me and Virtual Slideshow.

In regards to the first, we love quotes. These may be profound, pithy or humorous. A few powerful words can have a tremendous impact. For anyone who has felt utterly alone in their struggle or faced discrimination, for example, there's this one from Mahatma Gandhi: "Even if you are a minority of one, the truth is the truth." When somebody hears that at the right time in the right context, it can be very impactful.

We can learn a lot from listening to the wisdom of others. A single quote may inform the choices we make or even the direction we choose to go. One of my favorite quotes is from a mentor of mine who said, "A choice of words is often a choice of worlds."

The first of the two closing exercises I want to share recognizes the impact quotes can have.

4. You Can Quote Me

The idea with this exercise is to flip the script. It's not about reacting to a quote but saying something quotable.

My cofounder at We and Me, Will Wise, and I have noticed the impact quotes have on people in our work. Sharing a quote can spark meaningful conversation, increase critical thinking and raise engagement in a way that a simple prompt won't. To leverage that, I created a deck of *We! Engage Cards* with quotes (and images) on them.

Frequently, we read quotes from people who are famous, well-known or an authority on a topic. Maybe they've written a book. There's some reason they're quoted. As such, we might think only certain high profile individuals, or dead people, can be quoted. The truth is there's no reason that every member of your team can't be quotable if that's their intention.

That's how I frame this closing exercise. I ask people if they can summarize the entire meeting we've just had in one quote. Then I invite them to do this by unmuting and sharing, putting their quote in chat on a virtual platform or jotting it down on a sticky note and holding that up to the screen.

The intention here is to sound wise, eloquent, witty or funny—whatever suits you. Just write down a quote that summarizes the meeting. It's super simple, quick and powerful.

Sidebar: You Can Start Your Meeting With Most of These Exercises Too
Although I'm framing these as closing exercises, many can become starter exercises as well. You just need to adapt them, make little changes or tweak the framing. Then kick off your meeting with these exercises to put connection over content.

You can also use these exercises as a kind of attention reset. This will help you move from a consumption model to a contributor mindset.

5. Virtual Slideshow

For this exercise, there's actually no screen-sharing required. You won't be doing a PowerPoint, using Google Slides or anything like that. Virtual Slideshow utilizes the speaker view feature in Zoom. With this platform, whoever is speaking shows up big on everyone's screen.

You can tie this exercise into Application Anchors, described above. At the end of your meeting, you can have each team member "check out" by sharing something with the group.

Go alphabetically by first name so you don't have to spend time deciding on the order, or let people share as they feel called to do so. Invite each group member to share, in speaker view, an intention. Have everyone hold up an object that relates to what they're sharing.

You could have everybody grab an image that represents one takeaway from the meeting. Alternatively, team members could share an image that represents what they want to accomplish at the next meeting.

As they share, invite them to cover most of the screen with that object or image. In speaker view, it will look almost like a slide, and you have the team member live-narrating in the background. When that person is done, the next team member holds up their image or object and talks about what it represents to them to keep the Virtual Slideshow moving.

You can also ask each person to snap their fingers when they unmute and that'll cue Zoom to make their screen big which adds a nice little audio transition.

If you're used to being in gallery view, you know people just look like tiny pixelated boxes. Utilizing speaker view is a great way to increase a sense of connection and bring your team together.

ONLINE LEARNING

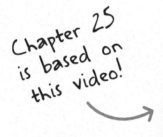

Chapter 25 is based on this video!

Máté 2 weeks ago

Finally a video that has real content. Good job, Chad. Thanks for that!

   REPLY

Chad Littlefield 2 weeks ago

Ha! YES! The only type of fluff I like is marsh-mellowy and goes on a sandwich. Glad you found value in the video. I share weekly videos on the channel. And I try to only create content I would be interested in watching. Every video title is an exact question that somebody has asked verbatim in one form or another. I try to give the answer justice in less than 5-12 minutes.

  REPLY

25

How to Be Interactive in a Virtual Presentation

3 Secrets to Breaking the "Sage-on-the-Stage" Dynamic in a Virtual Presentation

My job is most people's biggest fear: public speaking. I've traveled around the world and spoken to tens of thousands of people virtually and in person. I've had the opportunity to share my ideas on the TEDx stage and with some of the top organizations in the world. That means I've also had plenty of opportunities to fail and learn from those mistakes.

As the writer James Joyce once said, "Mistakes are the portals to discovery."

I believe a presentation should feel more like a conversation. In my work, I've had to develop ways to make virtual presentations more interactive.

So I'm going to share three secrets that help me give really interactive, engaging presentations. I'm not a big fan of the "sage-on-the-stage," let-me-speak-at-you approach.

Here are three ideas you can implement right away to make your presentations much more interactive.

Secret No. 1: Don't Use PowerPoint—Unless You Really Must

Everyone uses PowerPoint. You'll stand out by choosing a more engaging alternative. A slide presentation puts people in a certain "business as usual" mindset. Your audience will expect to just be a consumer and take in what you have to say passively. So if you must use PowerPoint, at least don't start with it.

I'm certainly not saying you shouldn't use visuals, which can be powerful. My preference, though, is analog visuals. I love holding up quotes to the screen that frame where we're going, and using props—like say a rubber heart, since public speaking often increases people's heart rate. That's going to be so much more visceral and memorable than just using PowerPoint.

For a TEDx Talk I did with Will Wise, my co-founder at We and Me, we brought a big sign on stage with the words "Listening to Understand." For really important ideas, consider printing them out. Turning your words into a visual can be more engaging than simply conveying your message verbally.

Going a step further to interact with my audience, sometimes I will "break the fourth wall"—an idea from theater. You can do this presenting in a boardroom or conference room or on a big stage in front of 8,000 people.

> **Turning your words into a visual can be more engaging than simply conveying your message verbally.**

In theater, what happens on stage usually stays on stage—you don't generally interact with the audience. But the moment an actor, character or performer turns to the audience and says, "Hey, you," they're breaking the fourth wall. When you do this, you can see people react, and they become much more alert and focused on what you're saying.

Secret No. 2: Use Cards or Analog Props Your Audience Can Access

Although you're using these for virtual meetings, you still want your cards or props to be something others could touch and feel if you were in the same place.

I've created a deck called We! Connect Cards that have questions on them to spark interaction and connection. For example, "What is something kind that someone else has done for you recently?"

and "What are you grateful for?" Going back to secret No. 1, if it's important enough—like asking my audience, "What brings you joy?—I print out a giant poster and bring it on stage with me.

You can access a free printable version of the *We! Connect Cards* on our website, www.weand.me, or you can purchase a deck. Use these visuals with your group to promote connection before content.

I also use quotes from a deck we compiled called *We! Engage Cards* in my virtual presentations and videos. These have quotes on one side and pictures on the other. They're really useful to create what one of my favorite facilitators, Jennifer Stanfield, calls "shielded discussion." The cards serve as prompts, helping people get to know each other in a non-threatening way.

If you want your presentation to be interactive, you've got to invite people to contribute, rather than just consume material. To do that, you might lay out all the cards—picture side face up. If you don't have the deck, lay out a bunch of images. Then tell everyone to grab an image that represents one unique thing you bring to the team.

> If you want your presentation to be interactive, you've got to invite people to contribute, rather than just consume material.

You see how I'm making my presentation about others in the group, not about me.

Going back to the first TEDx Talk I was ever invited to give on the topic of "Positive Social Risk," I did something a little bit edgy—I threw things at the audience. Boxes. Fairly big ones. People may have assumed I was calm and confident. But what you might not have known if you were in the audience, is that the minutes—and days—before the talk, I was about as nervous as I've ever been in my entire life. I've since come to learn why.

I was nervous because before my talk, all I was thinking about was one person—me. Even into the first 30 seconds of the talk, I was totally focused inwardly on myself. I wondered, "Will people like this?" "Will they like me?"

At some point, however, my perspective shifted. I remembered that this is for the audience—the collective *we*—this is for the group. Throwing boxes (which represented a perceived social barrier that isolates us from other people) into the audience was my way of really pulling them in and engaging the audience. It was a way to say to everyone all at once, "I see you."

If you're not using the *We! Engage Cards* I mentioned, you could print your own materials. The idea is to have something tactical and tangible that prompts interaction or conversation. This is an amazing way to create shielded discussion that increases psychological safety and is really phenomenally interactive for a group.

Once, before leading a workshop for a group of CEOs in Philadelphia, I went to Glassdoor and pulled a bunch of online reviews from their companies, printed them and cut out things their employees said. My intention was to make the session deeply personalized and interactive. I wanted them to identify why people stayed at their companies and why people left.

I could have just told them that because I already read all the reviews and analyzed the data a bit in preparation for the session. But I knew that if I did that, they would be much less likely to remember and retain that information and actually do anything about it. Using the little cutout paper versions of their reviews, I told them they had 15 minutes to sort the printed comments into two different buckets and figure out why people were staying at their companies and why people were leaving.

You can do something equally interactive virtually by using any digital whiteboard. Create a bunch of sticky notes. Have the group sort them out into two different buckets. If you're trying to teach definitions, you can have the words on one side and the definitions on the other, and have the group learn the same vocabulary together.

There are so many things you can do when you've got materials you can separate and use in interactive ways.

Secret No. 3: Use the Popcorn Method

The best way to avoid awkward silence is to create productive silence. To turn this idea into action, I regularly use what I call the popcorn method.

Think about making microwave popcorn. Save for the hum of the microwave, it's quiet until POP! Then a moment later, POP, POP, POP, POP, POP, POP! The momentum is exciting. But you've probably learned you have to stop heating it before the pops slow down too much or there's space between the pops. If you don't it'll burn. As I've said before regarding when to wrap up meetings or take breaks, you want to end the party while it's still fun. In the same way, you don't want to wait for responses beyond the time it's fun for the group.

Practically, this looks and sounds a bit like making microwave popcorn.

I ask the audience one question, say, "What did you notice about the conversations you just had?" or "What did you notice about the last three slides that I just shared?" or "What stuck out to you about the last 10 minutes of what I shared with you?" I'll tell everyone that I'm giving them 10 seconds to think about their responses, and then I want them to quickly "popcorn out" a bunch of answers. The point is to avoid eliciting that one long, two-minute answer, and make sure you're getting rapid-fire answers to bring in more voices, more energy and more momentum.

At any point, you can invite someone to elaborate on your quick response. You can add some "butter" to their popcorn by offering your perspective or share what thoughts their response sparked for you. This is a powerful way to affirm that you heard someone and to implicitly reward the group for taking the risk to share.

To Review

Don't use PowerPoint ideally, and if you must, don't use it in the first few minutes. Instead, kick off your presentation with a question, a prompt or an activity.

If you can, use cards or some other materials you can separate that are tangible. One way I encourage this virtually is by inviting people to grab an image off Google Images and paste that link into the chat. Remember, if the group isn't doing anything, you might be interesting, but they're not actually interacting yet.

Then, we have the popcorn method. Ask the group a question, let everyone think on it and then get a bunch of responses quickly.

The advanced version of the popcorn method that I love—and which you may or may not be comfortable trying—involves riffing off what your audience says.

I think the best presentations contain an element of improvisation, where you hear something from the audience, and then respond with a related story, statistic or example. When I do this, I might share something, and we go down that rabbit hole just for 30 seconds or a minute, and then we come back.

The goal is to turn a one-way presentation into a two-way conversation. By following these three tips, you can make any virtual presentation much more interactive.

Chapter 26
is based on
this video!

 Andrea 7 hours ago

Learning is a deeply social process, hence there is no way distance learning might exceed the in-person experience. But distance learning can be very effective, impactful, engaging and fun, too, by adopting your excellent suggestions. Great tips!

    REPLY

 Chad Littlefield 3 hours ago

I think in-person learning is superior ... for some learners. Context is everything. With the right content, I see the potential for distance learning to give meaningful access to education to adult learners and others that may not have the opportunity to make in-person learning a reality. Thanks for commenting, Andrea! I appreciate you sharing and look forward to continuing the conversation in future videos.

   REPLY

26

How to Make Distance Learning Fun

6 Techniques You've Got to Try

Distance learning is still learning. As such, you don't want any loss to happen because there's space between you and the learner. That's why it's important to make the experience enjoyable.

As part of my job, I help some of the top universities in the world make connection and engagement easy, so they can improve distance learning. My secret mission is to make distance learning even better than in-person learning. Whether that is possible or not is actually beside the point for me. It's a mindset that allows me and the faculty and staff that I work with to push the limits of what is possible in a distance learning context.

If you're wondering what you can do to make distance learning phenomenal, here are six techniques I'd suggest.

1. Encourage students to test online platforms.

According to Maslow's Hierarchy of Needs, a motivational theory in psychology, we're driven by things like physiological needs, safety, love or belonging, self-esteem and finally, self-actualization, or realizing our potential. But in the modern age of distance learning I'd add one more need to the bottom of the hierarchy: Wi-Fi. Can you actually get connected?

Below is the internet's wonderful and humorous adaptation of Maslow's classic framework.

Kidding aside, you can't learn online without internet connectivity. If it's your first time logging into a particular video platform or your students' first time and they don't know what to do, that's not useful.

One of the easiest ways to make distance learning fun is to make a game of exploring a new virtual space. I do that by actually inviting students to try their hardest to break a platform. Now I'd be very cautious about what group of students I'd suggest this with because some might succeed. But I frame it as encouraging students to explore. Try to post an entire book in the chat. Click on all the buttons or features on a platform at the same time as quickly as possible.

The only guideline I would give students is to not press the "end" or "leave meeting" button.

Tech prep and practice is really important, because without that you're not going to have fun distance learning. You're going to have *frustrating* distance learning.

> One of the easiest ways to make distance learning fun is to make a game of exploring a new virtual space.

2. Give students voice and choice.

Typically, we think about distance learning as a consumption model. Students just consume everything you're throwing at them. But that's not fun and engaging learning. What's fun and engaging is being able to contribute your thoughts and perspective—and to feel seen, heard and possibly understood in the process.

Think of it this way. Do you feel more energized after binge-watching Netflix for five hours or working hard building, fixing or creating something?

For most people, more effort brings higher reward when it comes to learning. At least that's the case if—and this is a really important qualifier—that effort is moving toward a larger purpose for them. That could involve striving toward a career goal. or another personal objective. The consumption model on the other hand is very low effort, and it rarely leads to high reward—or retention for that matter.

To give students voice and choice, you have to design your content for contribution.

3. Connect before diving into content.

The easiest way to design for contribution—and a really impactful approach to make online distance learning fun—is to connect before you get into content.

> The easiest way to design for contribution—and a really impactful approach to make online distance learning fun—is to connect before you get into content.

So often we just dive straight into the content and students and instructors don't connect. My wife got her master's online and had a really bad experience with group work that lasted the entire semester. This was partially caused by the instructor diving right into content. There was no personal connection. As a result, there was also no accountability or reliability.

If you're hoping your students self-organize to collaborate on a project throughout your program, you absolutely must carve out some time to facilitate connection between students. Great leaders and educators assume the social risk for their students to make meaningful connections.

That's the approach you'll want to take to make sure students engage. Throughout the book, you'll find many clever methods and strategies to facilitate this connection before content.

4. Blend analog with digital.

When you're sharing anything on camera or doing something synchronous and you interact with your space, it changes everything. It's like you're not trapped in this tight frame anymore. You're breaking the fourth wall—as it's described in theater—and interacting directly with your audience.

Just mixing it up with a pinch of visual novelty will pleasantly surprise learners and reset their attention. You could pop out from behind the camera or appear from beneath a table at the start of a session. When you reach behind your space to grab a book off a shelf or an object to tell a story, it's really engaging. Blending analog elements with the digital experience makes the whole exchange more dynamic.

Oftentimes, when I'm laying out my agenda for a workshop, it'll actually be a series of objects placed in a particular order on my desk. Each object will represent either a story I'm going to share, an activity we're going to do, a question I want the group to answer in the chat, or a point I'm trying to make. When I do that, I don't actually look at a screen or use PowerPoint slides. This method of introducing my learners to several different analog items that exist "off camera" for them creates a curiosity gap. People start to wonder what's coming next.

5. Make sure your camera is at eye height.

You don't want to be looking down at your students. That feels really terrible and condescending. You also don't want to go into Oompa-Loompa mode, where your laptop screen is pushed back and your students can only see the top half of your head along with a few prominent nose hairs. You want to be at eye height with your camera.

Let's say you're on Zoom, Google Meet or any other virtual platform. I often invite people to treat the camera lens as the friend of your best friend. You might not want to stare at it the entire time because that can be a little intense. And it's hard to sustain passion and energy for an extended period when you are just staring into a black hole that is not giving you any feedback. You may want to be tuned into the camera for some things, but also be looking down to see what students' reactions are and what people might be saying in chat.

Sometimes the camera acts like a black hole. You know, that region of spacetime where gravity is so strong that nothing—no particles or even electromagnetic radiation such as light—can escape from it. OK, perhaps it's not quite that intense, but your camera does have the ability to suck out your energy. You don't want to be exhausted at the end of the day when you're facilitating distance learning. If you're drained, the next class you have to teach is going to be rough.

If you happen to be pre-recording content, I'd highly suggest recording in bulk and handing the footage off to an editor to tighten it up and add some crop cuts or jump cuts. Student brains are adjusted to this fast-paced editing, so a 40-minute lecture recorded from one lame angle is *not* going to be fun, engaging or effective.

6. Use your space and sound.

When you're talking about ideas or sharing stories, move across your space. When you return to a story or idea, step back to the space where you started that thought.

You can play with this in some funny ways in a virtual context by moving closer or further away from your camera and mic. This visual and audio mix-up creates another helpful attention reset. Monotone talking heads don't make distance learning fun. But pulling out a bell or a noisemaker right before you are about to make the most important point of the class primes students' brains to tune in and remember what happens next.

Beyond that, I like to stand when I'm leading a virtual workshop. But if I'm leading a Q&A or an ask-me-anything segment, I like to sit. It feels a little bit less formal, and you can hang back and chat.

When you shift state like that, it changes people's script and the way that they experience learning. If you haven't taught standing up—and your knees will let you—try it before you knock it. I had a faculty member who was remarkably resistant to standing in front of his computer. But he tried it one Monday morning and emailed me afterward exclaiming how struck he was at the impact it had on *his* energy levels, not to mention the students' engagement.

You can apply all these things creatively and adapt whether your distance learning is synchronous or asynchronous. If you want more resources, there are a ton at our website www.weand. me/free. Use these to make online learning and engagement fun and easy for you and your students.

Chapter 27 is based on this video!

Mario 5 days ago

I can't thank you enough. I've been a trainer and life coach for 10 years, but this virtual approach feels so new to me. Your videos are awesome and not only helpful but make 100% sense to my facilitator brain. Thanks a lot! I have a big meeting of almost 120+ people. Trust me, I tried to reduce the size. Anyway, got any tips for this size of crowd?

   REPLY

Chad Littlefield 5 days ago

So glad to hear it, Mario! I use all the things I share here regularly in sessions of 300+ people via Zoom. Just needs some small adaptations. You might enjoy these seven do's and don'ts: https://youtu.be/hepSa-EHUjM

  REPLY

⇒ 27 ⇐

How to Facilitate Cooperative Learning in a Team

8 Cool Ways to Kick Off a Class or Meeting

Did you know that there are more than 28,000 three-second moments that happen every single day? The thing is, we totally forget the vast majority of them.

In this chapter, I'm going to unpack eight really cool opening lines or ways to start off a meeting, class, workshop or training exercise to make an impression and answer the question: How do you facilitate cooperative learning?

We gain so much wisdom by learning from the group. But how do we pull all that together? These methods I'm going to tell you about actually came from a client. I worked with a few hundred faculty, instructors and staff at Ohio State University. Afterward, Brian Raison, a professor at the university, shared this great list. He calls it "Tips for Teaching: Great Opening Lines for Impact." I thought it was just such a beautiful compilation that I'm going to share my own take on it.

For each tip on the list, I'll give you a concrete example for how to apply it from my own teaching and facilitation with some of the top universities and organizations on the planet. When I'm leading a group and have 300 people on Zoom, I am really deliberate about the first three seconds. I want what I say to be memorable, and that helps facilitate cooperative learning, bringing people together to create this atmosphere where they want to engage and learn from each other.

Another faculty member at OSU says you do 90% of your teaching in syllabus week, the first week of a semester, in the culture that you set. If you don't set the foundation for cooperative learning, you can expect that it won't happen for the rest of the semester.

Here are the eight ways to lead off a class, inspired by Brian Raison and my own experience:

1. Start with a startling statistic, surprise or unexpected fact.

2. Open with a quotation.

3. Use a thinking analogy.

4. Ask a rhetorical or challenging question.

5. Deploy a quiz or survey.

6. Tell a personal story.

7. Note the occasion.

8. Bring a prop.

1. Start with a startling statistic, surprise or unexpected fact.
I began this chapter with a startling statistic. You probably hadn't considered that there are nearly 30,000 three-second moments every day, and we forget 98% of them. That attention-grabbing stat turns on people's brains.

2. **Open with a quotation.**

I find this one immensely useful and extremely easy to implement. In the very beginning, you want to create some kind of context hook that engages people and activates their brains.

> In the very beginning, you want to create some kind of context hook that engages people and activates their brains.

I use the deck of *We! Engage Cards* that we created. The quote I'll often open up with to facilitate cooperative learning is an idea from Bill Nye The Science Guy: "Everyone you will ever meet knows something you don't." The moment I say that it changes the context for any breakout session that I might do on Zoom as well as any in-person interaction.

Everyone in your group, no matter whether they're younger or older, or have less experience or more, has something in their brain that you don't have in your own.

The *We! Engage Cards* have quotes on one side and images on the other. There are a ton of really cool cooperative learning exercises to get people connected and engaged in a way run-of-the-mill meetings won't. You can go to our website www. weand.me/free to download a free digital version of the cards or order the actual deck and have it shipped to you.

By sharing a quote, you can immediately set the tone or provide context in a learning environment. Pick whichever quote speaks to the environment you want to create in that moment.

3. Use a thinking analogy.

Analogies and metaphors are so powerful because they make things that are abstract or seemingly irrelevant directly relevant to your students or team. You're referencing something that's familiar to help them grasp a new concept.

4. Ask a rhetorical or challenging question.

I do this often. I wrote a book with Will Wise, my co-founder at We and Me, called *Ask Powerful Questions: Create Conversations That Matter.* Oftentimes, if I'm leading a workshop on the book, I find it's fitting to start with a question.

I might ask, When you meet someone for the first time, what questions do you typically ask? Even in a crowd of hundreds or thousands online in a class or webinar, I'll invite people to quickly share questions we typically ask.

What I get back is, How are you? Where are you from? What do you do? Even in a group of a thousand, we come up with the same four to five questions right off the top of our heads.

I've now invited the group's perspective into that cooperative learning. It's like saying let me learn from you. Let me live out that quote from Bill Nye. You can focus on questions that break outside that routine-question rut.

The example that Brian uses that I really appreciate evokes emotion. In this case, he asks that students do NOT raise their hands in response to make it a little more psychologically safe. He asks, "In your minds, raise your hand if you know the feeling of having blue flashing lights show up behind you when you're driving?" Then he asks students to imagine that immediate adrenaline rush or whatever you're feeling.

If you're in a biology or psychology class, that question is a great way to begin talking about the fight-or-flight response or to introduce the region of the brain called the amygdala. It's something that resonates with people.

5. Deploy a quiz or survey.

I'll actually invite people to raise their hands to respond to a survey.

I'll ask, for example, if students have any siblings, nieces, nephews or kids who are about 3 to 5 years old. Of course, there's always somebody who doesn't. They're 22 and single and don't have a big extended family. If I see everybody doesn't have their hand raised, I'll ask a follow-up question to introduce a little humor. How many of you at some point in your life were a little kid? Then everybody's hand goes up.

This provides a little levity, helps students engage and sets the tone really well for what I'm going to share next in that workshop. In that case, I might talk about the way our brains develop.

If you know a kid who's 3 to 5, you know they constantly ask why. Our brains get really rooted in the pathway of asking why questions. But in the book *Ask Powerful Questions*, we invite people to cut why out of their vocabulary. Instead, ask questions that only begin with how or what.

This is a great way to connect and come across as less judgmental when you're talking with someone new. If the aim is to build a relationship of trust with another person, it helps to let go of why questions.

With my example question, I'm engaging students by talking about how their brain developed when they were 3 to 5.

That is personalizing learning in a beautiful way.

6. Tell a personal story.

I don't really understand all the neuroscience or psychology behind why our brains are so wired for stories. Since humans have existed, we gathered in circles and around fires and told stories. Before the written word, we had word of mouth.

There's just something in our brains that loves stories. I witness this when I'm speaking in a virtual context and in person. The group leans in when I'm sharing an idea and I start telling a story.

> **There's just something in our brains that loves stories.**

One story I often share is this: 15 minutes before I got married, I was asked one of the most powerful questions I've ever gotten. It changed the way I experienced that day, and even the nature of my relationship with my wife. Right away, you want to know, what was the question? (For the answer, read the chapter on "How to Motivate Virtual Teams" earlier in the book.)

A good suspenseful story creates that curiosity gap. And when we hear a story, we relate to people.

One thing I'd add is a personal challenge I've accepted. I try to share my own failures, missteps and mistakes, and other people's successes. That's because those stories are way more relatable than if you just say look how awesome I am, and count the ways. That's part of the reason I wanted to highlight Brian's eight tips, instead of just drawing from my own experience.

I actually keep a log of my failures and missteps, a failure resume. I have a Google Doc I update for this. Every time I make some stupid mistake or do something that doesn't land very well, I add it to my failure resume. Then anytime I need to pull in a story or an opening line for a workshop, I can go to that story bank to cue my brain.

7. Note the occasion, and state the intention.

I've added the "state your intent" piece to this suggested opening tip. If we gather and the intention isn't crystal clear from the very beginning, we risk getting way off course.

8. Bring a prop.

This is especially valuable in virtual learning. The brain is wired to take in visual data and encode it into long-term memory.

If I'm kicking off a workshop and we're going to be digging into questions on listening from *Ask Powerful Questions*, I might immediately start off by talking about how ears have the ability to change what happens in your brain. I'll use visuals of an ear and a brain to illustrate the impact of listening. That makes it more likely people will remember what I'm teaching.

Props are cool, too, if you're in a virtual context. I had a client who I was coaching around storytelling at a big annual company conference. We were on Zoom, and he had this really cool background. I asked him if there was any item on his back wall that had a story behind it he could tell. Sure enough, he had an intricate mask from South America and a flag from his grandfather that he pulled off the wall during his message to bring closer to the camera. This allowed attendees to feel like they were interacting with his space a bit more.

By the way, you can actually combine any or all of the eight techniques above. I might reach behind me if I'm on Zoom and grab my throwable microphone and talk about Catchbox, the engagement microphone, and the awesome work that they do creating audience engagement. I could use this object to talk about how I interact with an audience to break that sage-on-a-stage dynamic.

When you interact with your space, everything comes to life, engages people's curiosity, and makes your team meeting more dynamic.

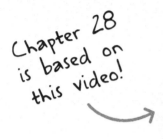

Chapter 28 is based on this video!

Tepedino 4 days ago

I have learned so much from Chad and Will in the last couple of months! I will be putting all that I've learned into practice starting this week with my student leader training sessions! The one online learning tip that I have found helpful is to hide my own video, which can reduce exhaustion and make me less self-conscious.

    REPLY

28

How to Make Online Learning Fun

Don't Just Show or Tell—Do

I've written a lot about ways to make connection and engagement easy in a virtual context. For this chapter, I want to specifically unpack how to make online learning really fun.

I'm going to keep it short and share a simple but brilliant framework. Understanding and applying this will go a long toward making virtual learning more enjoyable for your students— whoever they are. The most important thing to remember to make online learning fun is to *do* rather than just show.

> The most important thing to remember to make online learning fun is to do rather than just show.

I was working with a university career center, helping them transform a two-day, in-person academy boot camp that they had for sophomores into an all-remote, online learning context. They were so excited about the in-person program. It was going to be experiential and hands-on. The flow was built to be fun. But after learning they had to do it all virtually, they felt let down.

When they came to me, I encouraged them to change the way they looked at this shift to an online learning context.

There's so much opportunity with virtual learning *because* everybody is on their device, with access to the internet—which holds a library of infinite information. In about seven keystrokes, you can find anything you want and learn more about it.

Learning by Doing

There's so much learning that can happen by doing. Specifically for this group, one of the things we talked about was a resume writing workshop. Originally, they were going to have everybody print out their resumes for the boot camp, so they could get feedback in person. There was movement and live feedback. It felt dynamic.

We talked about using virtual breakouts and screen-sharing. Students could share their resumes as a Microsoft Word document or through Google Docs or another program, and have their resume edited live. They could make changes based on feedback from a coach, all online. Students could actually leave the workshop with a polished, edited resume; whereas in person, they'd leave with just one more thing to add to their to-do list.

Can you imagine how lousy an online learning course would feel if it was just telling you how to create your resume?

Some showing is fine. These chapters and my YouTube videos are showing rather than doing because it's asynchronous learning.

But when you're synchronous, you can invite people into an

experience, rather than just talking about maybe doing things later. With that in mind, we transformed that resume writing workshop into an experience where everybody would actually end up with a polished resume that they could use to land an internship or job.

> I find with that intention and just a pinch of creativity, you can radically redesign your content for contribution, not just consumption.

That kind of breakthrough created what I would call "deep fun" in online learning. The satisfaction that a student gets from making real progress toward a career goal or an objective they've set for themselves is irreplaceable. The more we keep both in balance, the more engaging our online learning will be. Next time you go to teach a concept, ask yourself, "how could we *do* this live with the group?"

I find with that intention and just a pinch of creativity, you can radically redesign your content for contribution, not just consumption.

Chapter 29
is based on
this video!

TssElective 7 hours ago

Your stuff is fantastic—going to share with my teachers, because as you said, low-hanging fruit. Shout out to the friend who introduced me to you— and can't wait to someday actually get to one of your conferences.

    REPLY

Chad Littlefield 3 hours ago

Many thanks for the kind words! So glad that our paths have crossed! I send out lots of free, low-hanging fruit once a week here as well FYI: https://weand.me/free.   And I try to answer as many questions as possible in the comments, so ASK away. 😊

  REPLY

Josh 1 weeks ago

These are so great! I'm literally going to use the Jamboard and renaming your profile today in less than one hour for teaching my class via Zoom. Thanks, man!

    REPLY

— 29 —

How Does Technology Make Learning Fun?

Improve Engagement While Minimizing Distraction With Backup Plan

Several years ago, I was at a conference on teaching and learning with technology where one of the keynote speakers went by the nickname of the "App-ologist." For her keynote, she had three giant foldout tables with every type of electronic device, laptop, phone, weird camera and digital tool. Her pitch was that she'd downloaded every single app, so she could tell you about the ones you needed.

Then she goes to play a video on a PowerPoint slide during her keynote and it freezes. Here is where she taught me one of the best lessons about how to make technology fun. She immediately looks up at the screen and notices that the video isn't playing. She acknowledges right away that the video isn't working, describes in brief what happens in the video, then moves on just as quickly to the next slide.

Many other presenters would have spent a minimum of a minute, and probably closer to five minutes, getting out of PowerPoint, trying to load it up, restarting a computer, and apologizing 15 times to the group. The lesson she taught me about how to make learning with technology fun: Be an App-ologist, not an "Apology-ist."

So often when something doesn't work, the first thing we do is say sorry. We even sometimes apologize before anything goes wrong just anticipating that there might be a glitch. I think we should instead channel the mindset of the App-ologist: If tech is getting in the way, move it out of the way or let it go.

Now, I'll give you a nightmare story of my own. I was giving a virtual keynote to a client with hundreds of people on the call. Because I present to big conferences in a remote context, I have two forms of internet, and I pay an arm and a leg to get the fastest internet possible. It's OK if a participant's internet lags a little bit and then catches up. But I can't have my internet failing, because that's 500 people's attention and time being wasted.

Sure enough, there was an outage that affected all of Pittsburgh as I was giving my keynote. But instead of letting it get to me, I channeled the wisdom of the App-ologist. I immediately took out my phone, which had cellular data, rather than relying on Wi-Fi or hardwired internet. I jumped on Zoom and did the rest of the keynote from my phone. I considered that a lesson to always have a backup plan when you're using technology.

If you need to use a particular tool, software or activity, it's OK to rely on it a little. But don't make it the only option. Know what you're going to do if it fails or somebody can't access it. The fewer digital distractions that you have as the leader or educator, the more valuable and fun the learning experience is going to be for everyone.

Here are five ways to use technology to make learning fun. Just remember to use technology *lightly*. You don't need to spend weeks learning new software, and you shouldn't rely too much on one app, program or type of software. If I'm using any tech at all, I always assume that it won't work for at least one person. Because that's generally true, I like to have an alternative so that they can still engage and get value out of our time together.

> The fewer digital distractions that you have as the leader or educator, the more valuable and fun the learning experience is going to be for everyone.

1. Use Existing Features to Be More Interactive

Utilize Zoom features or those on whatever platform you're already meeting to connect with your audience in creative ways. Chat, annotation, emoji reactions and the like are all just tools that can be used for creative purposes beyond the obvious.

For example, everyone has the ability to rename themselves. I was recently leading a workshop with 75 people, and I invited everyone to change their last name to the answer to this question: What would your closest friend say is your best character trait? I became Chad Curious, another participant became Jessica Loyal, and so on.

All of a sudden, a 2-D experience—learning through technology—became 3-D. Now when I saw Jessica, I knew she was loyal, not just a pixelated box. In the same way, you can use other platform features to add depth.

I also like to use the emoji reactions tool in Zoom. I do

it oftentimes as a way to reflectively listen and make sure the group feels heard and knows that I understand them. Someone once said to me that if you can articulate somebody's problem better than they can, they'll automatically trust you to solve it.

To make that idea come alive, I've been doing this listening exercise where I make some assumptions about the challenges, problems and struggles that any particular group I'm working with is facing. I say I'm just going to read off a list of issues that I think might be annoying or frustrating.

I ask participants to give the thumbs-up icon for each one they agree with, or if they have their video on, I might ask them to give me an actual thumbs-up. I might also instead ask them to type "yes" into the chat—some way of acknowledging whether I'm on the right track.

Sometimes the prompts I read off are actual quotes that I pull from a pre-event questionnaire.

For example:

- "It's exhausting virtually presenting to a bunch of black boxes (i.e., people without cameras on)."
- "I feel like I'm working twice as hard, but creating half the learning."
- "I know my students are multitasking in class and missing key information."

When you use the "reactions" tool in this way, your screen suddenly starts lighting up with visual symbols of people saying "me too," "I've experienced that," and "Yes!"

2. Use Emojis

Chats are typically only two colors: black and white. Boring! If you're in an asynchronous environment, comments are bland too.

> Chats are typically only two colors: black and white. Boring!

Before I'm teaching anything remotely, I'll copy www.getemoji.com into the chat and invite people to go there. I might suggest they search for an emoji that represents the state where they live, their personality, one that makes them laugh, or whatever prompt I choose. Consider a prompt that relates to the topic of the day.

You can have people add the emoji to their names on whatever platform you're using, or add an emoji in the chat or comments. You can even invite people to put together a cryptic message answering one of your questions with a string of at least three emojis.

Getemoji.com is searchable, so you can find something that will fit just about any theme. Emojis are a universal communicator. If a picture is worth a thousand words, I think an emoji probably is worth at least 40.

3. Wikipedia Game 2.0

I've detailed the Wikipedia game version 1.0 in a previous chapter and on my YouTube channel. (If you haven't yet subscribed, you should!) The Wikipedia game is going from point A to point B by only clicking on hyperlinks. No use of the keyboard whatsoever!

For example, the goal might be to get from the Genghis Khan Wikipedia page to the color blue Wikipedia page in as few clicks as possible, or as fast as possible.

Wikipedia game version 2.0. is content-specific. I came up with this while talking to my father-in-law, who is a biology professor. We were discussing how to weave the Wikipedia game into one of his classes. If he's teaching photosynthesis, for example, he could actually create a map to go from point A to B to C to D to E as quickly as possible and to have students track their path. You have to go from sunlight to water to dirt to carbon to nitrogen—whatever path you want to set.

You choose the words, and it could just be two words, depending on what content you're teaching. Whether you want to go from protein to RNA or something else entirely, pick words that relate to your content or your class that day. Then play the Wikipedia game 2.0 as a warm-up. It's a fun, competitive way to kick off class, and a quick little introvert-friendly energizer in the middle of a class.

Naturally, the student who gets from the "start page" to the "end page" in the fewest clicks—or the fastest—wins. Once a winner is declared, you can have them share the path they took to get there. Alternatively, you may want to have students record their path on a piece of paper as they go if your challenge to the group is to get there in the fewest amount of clicks.

4. Fun Fact

You can do this in the chat or use a virtual whiteboard with sticky notes. The goal is to have everybody share a unique or a fun fact about themselves anonymously, and have others just guess who posted it.

It's a pretty classic, regular, even semi-boring icebreaker in person. But when it's done using technology, there are some cool ways to make it fun. You can go onto Google Jamboard and have people create anonymous sticky notes with their fun fact. You see them all laid out there.

You can also invite all participants to change their name to the same emoji—just one symbol you put in the chat—and then type their fun fact right into the chat. That way you don't know who is who. Then you can have people guess who typed in a particular fun fact and come off mute to acknowledge when others got it right.

This invites personal sharing. It works really well at the very beginning of an online learning session to get comfortable with technology and create some connection before content.

5. Utilize *We! Connect Cards*

For those who have followed my work for any amount of time, you may be familiar with the *We! Connect Cards* that I created. These have questions on one side and actions on the other. They have suggestions for a bunch of really fun, connecting group activities.

One of my favorite activities using technology is to go on Google Jamboard or any other virtual whiteboard, paste a picture of a question, and then invite people to answer it in sticky notes. It's visually interesting, and a neat way to kick off a regular old boring, standing meeting.

After 10 weeks of Monday staff meetings, or a whole semester or class, you could have a whiteboard *filled* with neat connections from the group.

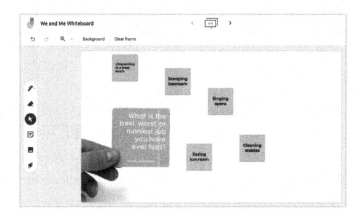

You might even make this your unofficial start to class. People will know if they log in early that they get to type in their answer to that question and maybe have some off-mute group sharing. This will invite some playful curiosity.

Now if you liked this chapter, you'll love the chapter on the "Do's and Don'ts of Virtual Meetings," earlier in the book. It's a really great summary of the best practices and worst things to do when meeting virtually.

Chapter 30
is based on
this video!

 The Magic Sauce   6 days ago

Man, so many teachers and trainers have to see this video. No more soul-destroying sessions!

     REPLY

 Dawn   4 days ago

The host sets the tone for a virtual meeting. An energized host creates energized engagement! ✵

     REPLY

30

The Quickest Way to Run an Online Q&A Session

This Won't Take Long to Explain

Having co-authored another book called, *Ask Powerful Questions: Create Conversations that Matter*, I'm especially intrigued at how the questions we ask shape the conversations we have.

One of my favorite ways to run an online Q&A session is what I call the "curiosity harvest." You can do this on any platform just using the chat. There are a few versions of the exercise, but the simplest is a two-step curiosity harvest.

Step 1: Harvest Individual Curiosity

Typically, when we run a Q&A session, we get to the end of a class, conference session, keynote or workshop and ask if there are any questions. Often when we do this, we run into a brick wall. No one asks any questions, or someone just blurts one out that's not helpful to the group.

A much more intentional way to handle this is to provide a bit of silence for people to come up with their question. I do this by having virtual participants open the chat and enter their question.

Invite them to rewind the tape on the meeting. What are they naturally curious about? What topic would they love to dive deeper into? What part of this person's expertise would they love to tap?

Then have them type a question related to that into the chat. *But have them wait to press enter.*

After about 10 to 30 seconds, tell your group that on the count of three you're going to have everyone hit "enter" at the same time. That will be the group's cue to blow up the chat with their questions.

That is round 1. You've harvested *individual* curiosity.

Step 2: Harvest Collective Curiosity

Next, harvest the group's collective curiosity. This makes for a way more useful, practical, engaging Q&A session online. What you don't want to do is have a presenter go down a rabbit hole with one rogue curiosity or question. You want to determine what the group is most curious about so that the leader can speak to as many people as possible.

> You want to determine what the group is most curious about so that the leader can speak to as many people as possible.

First, ask everybody to hit the CAPS LOCK button on their keyboard. Then, invite your group to read through everyone else's questions in the chat.

Their goal?

Read through everybody's questions, and retype a question that each person feels captures a theme from the group's collective curiosity. I might turn on some fun, upbeat instrumental music for this if you have over 20 questions in the chat.

I wait a moment for people to type in their questions and then have everyone press enter after counting down from three. As the facilitator or leader, I'm only paying attention to the questions in all caps to get a sense for what people *really* care about. This method is more engaging than simple "upvoting" of questions as it invites everyone to think deeply and tune into what the whole group cares about.

Then I pick a couple questions and lightning-round answer them, or I pick one question that's a really strong theme and have people discuss it in breakouts. My thinking, as I'll tell participants, is that the group collectively is *always* smarter than I am individually.

We might take this question: How do you motivate people on a remote team? I'll have everyone do a breakout for five minutes to answer that, and share what they learned with the larger group. Then I'll offer my perspective or thoughts *after* they've had a chance to share some of their ideas.

This is such a dynamic way to run an online Q&A session. It's way more interactive and participatory than other approaches. I've used this method with a group of three, 30 and 300. The mechanics just seem to work.

You can also invite us to come in and run a session on how to make virtual engagement easy for you. If you're interested, you can find more information on our website www.weand.me/virtual.

One fun alternative to running a Q&A session the way I described above is to pick a handful of questions from a deck of

We! Connect Cards. You'll find questions that nobody else will come up with but that everybody would really value to lead an engaging, and quick, online Q&A. This is a fun way for a guest speaker or presenter to do a lightning round Q&A.

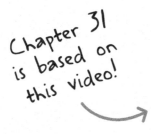

Chapter 31 is based on this video!

 Pamela   5 days ago

Hi Chad! I just became a facilitator for the company I work for where I am training new hires. Your channel is awesome, and I've learned a lot from you.

      REPLY

 Chad Littlefield   5 days ago

FANTASTIC! Love hearing this, Pamela. So glad you discovered the channel. I'll keep the videos coming 👍👍

      REPLY

⚡ 31 ⚡

Online Q&A Session
Best Practices

Try the Glasses and Chair Methods
to Engage with Your Group

I love powerful questions. But even more than that, I love helping people create conversations worth remembering.

In this chapter, I'm going to unpack the glasses method and chair method, which you can adapt and implement in your online Q&A sessions. These approaches are perfectly applicable whether you have 10 or 12 CEOs in a leadership group, 30 students in a classroom or 300 people at a virtual conference. Both the glasses and chair methods offer simple, subtle ways to create a totally different atmosphere for your Q&A session.

If you've ever attended a conference session with a Q&A or hosted one, you know that they can be really awesome—or abysmal. You can have that Q&A where 50 people line up in front of a microphone to ask their question. That usually turns into people nervously talking for two minutes before getting to their "question," which was really more of an opinion they wanted to share.

Ideally, you want people to ask crisp, powerful questions that let the presenter, speaker, panel or expert respond by sharing brilliant insights with the rest of the group. To do that, you've got to create a different atmosphere. This needs to be an environment that increases people's psychological safety. People tend to ramble when they're nervous.

> Ideally, you want people to ask crisp, powerful questions that let the presenter, speaker, panel or expert respond by sharing brilliant insights with the rest of the group.

The Glasses Method

I picked up the glasses method from a teacher-mentor named Matt Church. I don't even know if he was intentionally teaching this, but I observed it in what he was doing. Matt has been voted the top professional speaker in Australia. He's an amazingly dynamic, ultra-brilliant dude.

I was in a virtual workshop with him and he was lighting everyone's brain up with some fantastic ideas. Then he took a break, and he could see that the chat was filling up with questions. He needs glasses to read, so he put his on.

I don't know if he even noticed this, but this simple act had a very powerful effect. By putting on his glasses, he essentially let everyone know he was "listening." He was communicating to the group without a word that he was taking a break from sharing content to read through everyone's questions.

You don't need to wear glasses to use the glasses method. Rather, this is about developing a symbol or cue that makes it clear you are reviewing the group's questions. This is particularly useful if you want to try to embed Q&As throughout a session. If you have a two-hour training session, for example, you might not want to hold questions until the last 10 minutes. At the outset, let your group know they can type their questions in ALL CAPS into chat as they come up and if they want to dive deeper into a topic.

Then every handful of minutes pause briefly, and put on your glasses, don a "Q&A hat," start playing music, or commence with whatever your cue is. Basically just use a visual or audio cue of some kind to let your group know you're paying attention to them and going to take a moment to address their questions.

It might take 15 seconds for you to read five questions, which is still about 10 times faster than if you had five to 10 people verbally ask a question. You can run a very efficient online Q&A session this way.

The Chair Method

When I'm delivering virtual keynotes or holding remote workshops, it's really important for me to stand. I want my energy to come through as I'm presenting.

But there are instances when it makes sense to be a bit more relaxed, like for the Q&A. That's where the chair comes in. When I'm ready to open it up to questions, I'll let the group know, "I'm going to pull up my stool, so we can just have a chat." I will pull in my chair from outside the frame and have a seat. What I've noticed from hundreds of remote keynotes and workshops that I've led is something shifts in people's brains when I sit down. It creates a change of state. And as Matt Church often says, "State matters more than script."

My presentation style is extremely conversational and authentic. I don't put on an act. I'm just me. But there is just something about moving from standing to sitting down that feels like we're grabbing coffee together.

If you're in a conference room with a thousand people, I might look like this tiny dot at the front of the room. But if we meet in Zoom, I'm right there, up close and personal. It's as if we were having a one-on-one even if there are 493 other people online with us. It's amazing how intimate Zoom can feel when you're really intentional about how you use the tool.

Not an Afterthought

Now here's a little bonus tip: Your Q&A session should never be the last thing that you do. The Q&A should be the second to last thing.

> Your Q&A session should never be the last thing that you do.

When it's time, I'll pull up a chair to do the Q&A. But I'll finish that about five minutes before the meeting is over. Then I'll move the chair away. I'll say that I know there were some unanswered questions. And I'll let the group know that I'm going to send a video follow-up with more resources and answers to the questions we didn't get to during our Q&A.

After that, I'll transition to how I want to end the session. That might be with a story, activity or exercise. This closing is something really intentional. I might, for example, invite the group to quickly share some closing statements, aha's they had or actions they were excited to take.

Sam Keen once said that "Nothing shapes our lives so much as the questions we ask, refuse or ask or never dream of asking." Q&As can be really fun. But they typically have a more relaxed conversational energy. I want to end the meeting on a high note and infuse lots of energy into the group. To accomplish this, your Q&A should be the second to last thing you do, and you've got to be really deliberate with your closing.

If you're interested in more best practices to *Ask Powerful Questions* and *Create Conversations That Matter*, you can check out our other book on the topic at www.amazon.com/we. You can also get a free book excerpt through our website at www.weand.me/free.

Postscript

Got an unanswered question?

Just ask!

We trust your pixelated connections will be 10 times better than they were before you picked up this book. If that's not the case, we'd love to answer your lingering questions.

Nearly all of the chapter titles from this book are a real question asked by a real leader or educator. If you still have unanswered questions, please email them to us at hello@weand.me.

It's quite possible that your email will become the inspiration for a future video tutorial or even perhaps a new chapter in the second edition of this book.

Thanks for being a *Connector*!

Creating real connection and communication is hard.

*We help **leaders, educators** and **events** make it easy.*

About We and Me

Hi!

Chad Littlefield and Will Wise here, co-founders of We and Me, Inc.

Leaders call us when they want to amplify a culture of connection, belonging, and trust. Great leaders know that investing in their people boosts results and increases retention. We are mildly obsessed with relationships, organizational culture, learning & development, connection, trust, and team performance. We design and deliver interactive keynotes, team-building retreats, programs, and workshops that have real impact. And we've got the data to prove it. We'd be happy to share our success stories, whether helping tech startups like Typeform.com, Fortune 500 companies like JetBlue, or educational institutions around the world.

We believe...

- **Leaders accomplish more by asking powerful questions** than by commanding and controlling
- Deeper **human connection fosters more engagement** and **better performance**
- **People, purpose,** and **planet** are just as important as profit
- Interactive experiences have more impact than PowerPoint slides because **people learn by doing**

Not only do we believe these things, we are genuinely excited about making them a reality for each organization we work with.

Trusted by Educators, Businesses and Events Everywhere

jetBlue

Let us help you make *virtual connection* and *engagement* easy.

Invite us to...

Run a workshop on *How to Make Virtual Engagement Easy*

- Experience **5 Key Ingredients for Virtual Engagement**
- Learn **collaboration skills** your team can use that day
- Leave more **energized**—and less exhausted with concrete tools and strategies for engagment
- **Perfect for** university faculty and staff, educators, and leaders who are totally tired of bad Zoom gatherings

Run a **Virtual Connection Lab** to build your remote team

Host one session or a series to keep your team motivated and connected

- Build relationships that **inspire employees to stay**
- **Strengthen culture and morale** for your school or workplace
- Practice a set of (actually fun) **tools and strategies** you can use when on your own even after our sessions
- **Prevent burnout** with authentic (not cringy) connection

Speak at your virtual conference or event

We'll create and present a 60-minute interactive keynote and a 30-minute full-audience exercise (for 10 to 1000+ people)

- Kickoff your event with "Connection Before Content" **to build real community** to shatter the isolation of being remote
- Generate fresh ideas to **inspire your teams** at a distance
- Engage in ways that transform **ideas into action** immediately
- Absolutely 0 PowerPoint slides!

Contact us to explore availability, pricing, and working together.

www.weand.me   **hello@weand.me**

CHAD LiTTLEFiELD, MEd

Cofounder and Chief Experience Officer at We and Me Inc.

Photo credit to Erica Mueller

As a global keynote speaker and expert facilitator, Chad designs experiences and tools that build trust, strengthen connections, and unify your team. He helps break down communication barriers to make teams more cohesive, effective, and higher performing. He is a TEDx speaker and is also the author of the *Pocket Guide to Facilitating Human Connections*. He and Will are the cocreators of *We! Connect Cards™*, which are now being used to create conversations that matter within companies in over eighty countries around the world and on six of the seven continents. (Free deck if you live in Antarctica.) Chad lives in Pittsburgh, PA, with his wife and son, Kate and Otto, though they travel often for business and adventure.

WiLL WiSE, MEd

Cofounder and Chief Weologist at We and Me Inc.

Photo credit to Trish Hummer

Will Wise has been asking powerful questions for over two decades as a corporate development consultant, nontraditional school principal, university instructor, and team development thought leader. Will is also the cofounder of We and Me Inc. (www.weand.me), a company who partners with leaders and organizations to transform workplaces by establishing a culture of connection to save them time, increase productivity, and boost job satisfaction. He works with leaders to develop *who they are*—not just what they do. Will's clients have included JetBlue, TEDx, Typeform, NBC Universal, Penn State, and many others. He lives in Central Pennsylvania with his wife and three children.

Follow Will and Chad to receive actionable insights through their free interactive learning letter read by thousands of top leaders right here:

www.weand.me/ideas